the food of **Singapore**

Simple Street Food Recipes from the Lion City

by **David Wong & Djoko Wibisono**
photos by **Luca Invernizzi Tettoni**
introduction by **Lee Geok Boi**

TUTTLE Publishing
Tokyo | Rutland, Vermont | Singapore

Published by Tuttle Publishing, an imprint of Periplus
Editions (HK) Ltd

www.tuttlepublishing.com

Copyright © 2005 Periplus Editions (HK) Ltd.
All rights reserved.

ISBN: 978-0-8048-4510-6

*Previously published as The Authentic Recipes from
Singapore ISBN 978-0-7946-0229-1 pb*

Distributed by

North America, Latin America and Europe
Tuttle Publishing, 364 Innovation Drive
North Clarendon, VT 05759-9436 U.S.A
Tel: 1 (802) 773-8930; Fax: 1 (802) 773-6993
info@tuttlepublishing.com
www.tuttlepublishing.com

Japan
Tuttle Publishing, Yaekari Building, 3rd Floor
5-4-12 Osaki, Shinagawa-ku, Tokyo 141-0032
Tel: (81) 03 5437-0171; Fax: (81) 03 5437-0755
sales@tuttle.co.jp
www.tuttle.co.jp

Asia Pacific
Berkeley Books Pte Ltd
61 Tai Seng Avenue, #02-12, Singapore 534167
Tel: (65) 6280-1330; Fax: (65) 6280-6290
inquiries@periplus.com.sg
www.periplus.com

All recipes were tested in the Periplus Test Kitchen.

Photo credits: All photography by Luca Invernizzi Tettoni
except pages 7, 11, 18, 112 and endpaper by Edmund
Ho. Illustration on page 11 by Daniel Wegera.
Styling and food preparation: pages 32, 41, 58, 61, 91, 94
and 101 by Mrs Ong Kiat Kim and Christina Ong.

Acknowledgments: The publisher and Beaufort Sentosa
would like to thank the following for their generous
assistance in providing tableware, furniture and other
decorative items for use in this book: Abraxas; Blue
Moon; Tang's Studio and the Atelier. Thanks also to
the following restaurants for their kind cooperation in
arranging location photography: Hua Yu Wee Seafood
Restaurant, Komala Villas, Muthu's Curry Restaurant,
Alkaff Mansion, Aziza's Restaurant, Tai Thong
Restaurant and Li Bai Restaurant.

18 17 16 15 14   10 9 8 76 5 4 3 2 1

Printed in Singapore

Contents

Food in Singapore

A tropical metropolis with a voracious appetite

Situated at the tip of the Asian mainland, Singapore is an island nation that appears as but a tiny speck on the world map. From humble beginnings as a small fishing settlement 200 ago, it grew into an important British colonial entrepôt in the last century. And since becoming independent in 1965, Singapore has become one of Asia's most dynamic and modern cities with a GNP that rivals that of many larger nations.

Skyscrapers, expressways and air-conditioned shopping centres crammed with luxury goods from around the world replace the more traditional Asian vistas of paddy fields and palm-fringed beaches. Singapore's highly regulated system of government has produced the ultimate consumer paradise—a city which might, at first, seem lacking in passion and individuality. But when it comes to the subject of food, Singaporeans reveal their true identity—for food is, quite simply, the national obsession.

This is a country where food is a constant topic of conversation and no meal is complete without an extended discussion about the food being eaten or a recently enjoyed meal. Eating out is, for many, a daily routine and this habit has virtually created a national identity defined by the cuisine—especially the multi-ethnic fare served in unpretentious restaurants and hawker centres throughout the island. Here the food is prepared by self-employed chefs—often aided by family members—who once operated from temporary stalls along the roadside but have now been given permanent locations in food centres or upmarket air-conditioned food courts.

Few Singaporeans give much thought to the origins of what they are eating in this multi-racial society—what matters is the flavour. Typical Singapore food is actually a blend of many elements brought by the different immigrant groups who have settled here. Dinner could be Chinese-style soup and vegetables combined with a Malay chicken curry. Breakfast could be cereal and milk or Indian *dosai* with *dhal*. Even the methods of eating a meal are multi-cultural. One person sitting at a table may eat his rice with fork and spoon, and another with chopsticks, while a third person may use his fingers.

Singapore food is always accompanied by powerful sensations: garlic and shallots sizzling in a hot wok, sticks of satay grilling over an open flame, *belachan* (dried prawn paste) roasted before grinding, drops of ghee dancing on a hot griddle. These are some of the smells that trigger memories of home for Singaporeans, descendants of migrants who brought with them rich food traditions from all over Asia. There is in Singaporeans a spirit of adventure when it comes to food.

Money can buy you everything

Thanks to its location—just over 1 degree or about 140 kilometres (100 miles) north of the equator—Singapore is humid and steamy all year round. Tropical rains frequently bring freshness during the afternoons, and in contrast with the usually hot days, nights are balmy and the early mornings cool.

Dense equatorial rainforests and a few low hills which once shaped the landscape have long given way to an equally dense cover of high-rise office blocks, shopping complexes, condominiums and public housing. Now the tropical humidity and heat are kept at bay by air-conditioning, and the steel and concrete high-rise jungle is softened by numerous trees and small parks, which have earned Singapore the sobriquet "Garden City". Busy highways are divided by tall trees and flowering shrubs.

Amidst all this greenery, you would be hard put to find a farm, unless it's the indoor hydroponic variety or the few boutique organic farms. Singapore has grown almost none of its food for decades, preferring˄ to devote scarce land to industry and housing for its population of just over four million people.

However, money can buy you everything, and situated at the hub of a region that is still largely agricultural, Singapore imports its food and even its water from neighbours to the north and south. Since Southeast Asian markets do not carry all the produce and fine foods to which affluent, globe-trotting Singaporeans have become accustomed, its excellent air and sea connections bring in the best from around the world.

With produce now air-flown from everywhere, the island also marks the passage of the seasons around the world. The Thai and Indian mango season in April and May finds fruit shops here well-stocked with luscious and cheap mangoes. If it's summer and cherries abound in California, they do too in Singapore. Is it the season of the hunt already? Then premier restaurants around town will soon have game on the menu. And everyone knows when durians are in season. The pungent smell, fragrant or awful depending on how you feel about this thorny fruit, makes it hard to ignore. Garbage collectors certainly cannot ignore literally tons of thorny shells discarded daily.

Although seasonal foods mark the passage of spring, summer, autumn and winter in different parts of the world, few foods are ever out of season in Singapore, since

OPPOSITE: A bygone age of elegant dining is recaptured at the hilltop. Alkaff Mansion restaurant, formerly owned by one of the wealthiest Arab families in Singapore and now a posh dining venue with a view.

seasonal produce is flown in from countries both north and south of the equator.

Abundance does lead to a jaded palate. These days, with the average Singaporean becoming more and more well-travelled and well-versed in exotic cuisines from all over, food importers have to work extra hard looking for new and interesting products to tempt bored Singaporeans. The list of countries which supply Singapore with food products is growing constantly as buyers wander farther afield.

However, not everything consumed in Singapore is imported. The country does have a tiny group of farmers, some of whom grow leafy vegetables and fruits, while a few high-tech farmers cultivate their produce in multi-storied factories, growing vegetables hydroponically—without soil, in trays of nutrient-rich water and mushrooms in sawdust.

Both marine and freshwater fish, prawns and oysters are also farmed locally. Fish farmers have to work hard to keep up with the voracious demand for live seafood in restaurants. Being an island once inhabited by fishermen, it is no surprise that seafood is a popular and much loved item in the Singaporean diet. Seafood also escapes most religious strictures—Muslims do not eat pork; Hindus and strict Buddhists avoid beef and many Chinese find the taste of lamb and mutton a trifle strong.

While much of the daily demand for seafood is met by fishermen of the region, whose fishing boats unload their chilled catches in Singapore, the more expensive seafood such as sashimi-quality fish, huge meaty crabs, lobsters and other shellfish come in by air from as far away as Japan, Sri Lanka, France and Australia.

The abundance of quality produce gives creative cooks plenty to work with. The multi-ethnic population in Singapore are not only sources of culinary inspiration but also avid supporters of the country's food industry.

Creative restaurant chefs on the look-out for something new to excite the palates of Singaporeans are increasingly experimenting with new ingredients and new styles. Starting with a culinary heritage based on some of Asia's greatest cuisines—Chinese, Indian, Malay and Indonesian—they borrow from other Asian neighbours, experiment with Western ingredients and styles, mix something from here with something from there. Like everything else in Singapore, food is definitely on the move.

BELOW: These stalls, known locally as "zhu-chao" stalls, offer a basic range of dishes which can be cooked with the customers' ingredient of choice. One hot favourite is crab, either cooked with a sweet and spicy chilli gravy, served with bread, or with black pepper. RIGHT: A typical scene at a wet market in Singapore selling a wide variety of vegetables, meat, seafood, herbs, spices and cooked food from Indian, Chinese and Malay stall holders. These markets usually operate from the early hours in the morning to the early afternoon.

Eating Singapore Style

The search for culinary excitement continues

When Stamford Raffles, the British founder of modern Singapore, declared the little fishing village and occasional pirates' den a free port in 1819, he drew swarms of migrants in search of economic opportunities. The Chinese, especially from the southern coastal provinces of Fujian and Swatow, arrived by the boatload, following other Chinese who came to Singapore from settlements in nearby Java, Malacca and Borneo. The Indian community began with a small contingent of Indian soldiers in the British army. Not long after being declared a free port, Singapore was designated an Indian penal station and convicts were sent here to work on public buildings. British labour policy also brought in droves of Tamils from South India as indentured labour for public works projects.

The island's small Malay population swelled with newly arrived Javanese, Sumatrans, Boyanese from Madura and other Indonesian islanders, as well as Malays and Straits Chinese from Malaya. Arabs and Jews came from the Middle East; there was a fairly large community of Armenians and, of course, a strong enclave of Britons who administered the colony. By the end of the 19th century,

Singapore was perhaps the most cosmopolitan city in Asia. These migrants all arrived, by and large, from places with long-established culinary traditions. Now began the process of blending that has produced some of Singapore's most interesting dishes.

The hybridisation began the day a Malay girl married a Chinese man to form the first of the Straits or Peranakan Chinese families. Not all *babas* (Peranakan men) and *nonyas* (Peranakan women) had a Malay ancestor, but they were distinguished from the more recently arrived Chinese by the Malay dress of the womenfolk and by their cuisine. Straits Chinese or Nonya cuisine combined the Chinese affection for pork, prohibited to Muslim Malays, with Malay ingredients, such as coconut milk, fragrant roots and herbs, chillies and dried spices for character. Certain Chinese dishes, such as braised pork, were not ignored, but took on a local overtone with the addition of lemongrass and galangal, and many a bland Chinese dish was given a shot of pungent Sambal Belachan, a salty, spicy condiment of *belachan* (dried prawn paste) and chillies. Another community, the Eurasians—from the intermarriage of Europeans and Asians—also developed a hybrid cuisine that shares much with Straits Chinese cuisine but does not forget its European roots in its focus on roasts, steaks and chops seasoned with soy sauce and eaten with Sambal Belachan or chilli sauce. Neither does the community forget its Indian roots in certain dishes such as Vindaloo, a pork curry tarted up with vinegar, and Devil's Curry which, as its name implies, can set your tongue on fire.

Even without intermarriage, it is not possible to live cheek by jowl with someone of another ethnic community without picking up new food ideas. Perhaps surprisingly, the British, not noted for their cuisine, were also sources of inspiration. The colonial *memsahibs* employed Hainanese boys as cooks and they interpreted Western cuisine for their colonial masters in a way that produced Singaporean classics such as Hainanese Pork Chops: breaded pork cutlets fried in oil, then dressed with potato and tomato wedges, green peas and onions fried in a gravy of soy sauce thickened with starch.

Cuisines with more flourish than the British have also taken on multi-ethnic airs in Singapore. When a Singaporean thinks of Indian food, he thinks of Fish Head Curry, which is a dish that no one in India has heard of until he comes to Singapore. Indians may eat curry, but only the Chinese have the tradition of eating such things as heads, tails, ears and entrails. Mee Goreng, again prepared only by Singaporean Indians, is another Singapore Indian classic not found in India since the main ingredient, the starchy, yellow Hokkien noodles (*mee*), cannot be found there.

While Straits Chinese cuisine may be Chinese food with strong Malay overtones, local Malay food has also incorporated Chinese ingredients, such as noodles, bean sprouts, tofu and soy sauce. This has produced Singaporean Malay dishes such as Mee Soto Ayam (yellow Hokkien noodles served in a rich, fragrant chicken broth) and Tauhu Goreng, a delicious dish of deep-fried tofu stuffed with bean sprouts and slivers of cucumber, and topped with thick peanut gravy.

Chinese food itself has evolved its own distinctive Singaporean touches that show the influence of the other ethnic communities. Hainanese Chicken Rice may sound like it came from the Chinese island of Hainan. It was once indeed prepared only by the Hainanese in Singapore although you would be hard pressed to find it in Hainan, especially with that critical accompaniment of chilli sauce made with fresh ginger, chilli and vinegar.

While chillies may not be native to Southeast Asia, it is hard to imagine any Singapore-style noodle or rice dish without them. Every home and most restaurants stock chillies in one form or another, be it finger-length red sliced chillies, whole *chili padi*, green vinegared, or ground in a variety of sauces—regardless of race or culinary preference.

Singapore's prosperity is taken for granted by its huge middle class. With the wherewithal to travel beyond the confines of a very small country, to eat and drink well, they carry on the tradition of eating out that started when the menfolk did not have the time to do their own cooking and thus depended on itinerant hawkers. This practice is now fueled by the growing number of women working outside the home. Eating out and the constant exposure to good food have encouraged hybridisation of the cuisine, and the healthy competition has widened the range of new dishes created to tempt the ever adventurous epicure. The range of what people eat has grown tremendously. While a proper meal once consisted only of rice and side dishes—burgers, sandwiches, and pizzas go down just as well as noodles and rice. Singaporeans eat very eclectic meals with components or dishes from different cuisines—a habit encouraged by hawker centres and food courts. A typical food court meal may include Hokkien-style Popiah (spring rolls in soft wheat skins), Indian Sup Kambing (mutton soup) and a Chicken Chop.

With the different communities eating together, the host has to be mindful of religious strictures and choose food acceptable to all. Malay and Indian dishes pose no problems, and the highly adaptable Chinese food can now be found in *halal* Chinese restaurants conforming to Muslim dietary restrictions; these even attract Chinese customers who can now eat comfortably with their Muslim friends.

"Flexibility" and "opportunism" have been watchwords with the migrant communities from the beginning, and define the Singaporean mindset when it comes to the pursuit of economic advancement as well as eating. The resulting mix has livened up the Singapore food scene, enriching it with unique combinations that did not exist in the culinary traditions from which they stemmed.

OPPOSITE AND ABOVE: The recently restored Boat Quay and Clarke Quay areas along the Singapore River are ideal settings for alfresco meals.

Etiquette and Enjoyment

Whatever the ethnic community, and wherever the place, eating in Singapore is always communal. The assortment of dishes appear all at once, diners get individual servings of warm, fragrant rice and then help themselves to the side dishes. One exception to this is the Chinese banquet, a formal eight- or ten-course dinner, where the dishes appear one at a time.

"Don't use your fingers" is not an admonishment you will hear often. Indians, Malays and Straits Chinese will tell you that curry and rice taste best when you can literally feel the food with your fingers.

There are many interesting expressions and gestures that revolve around the dining table. Before the meal begins, it is considered polite to invite the more senior members at the table to eat. This harkens back to the Malay and Indonesian village tradition of inviting people present to partake in a meal. Members of the family often express their affection by dishing the choicest pieces into the bowls of their loved ones. Singaporean hosts—especially the older generation Chinese—would shudder at the thought of their guests leaving their dining table with their stomachs still hungry, and would rather pile their tables high with insurmountable portions of food. Note however, that guests who do not at least finish what is on their plate—down to the last grain of rice—are considered rude, so be careful how much food you place in yours!

Eating with your hand has its own etiquette, too. Only the right hand is used and just the fingers; the palm has to be kept perfectly clean. Washing the hands before eating is not only polite but hygienic. In finer Indian and Malay restaurants, a waiter will bring a bowl of warm water, sometimes with a lime, before and after a meal. In some Chinese restaurants, the bowl of delicately fragrant lime water is also a common sight whenever Chilli Crab or Prawns are served in the shell. There have been reports of unsuspecting tourists mistaking the water for a drink—so do warn your guests beforehand, especially if they are not familiar with Southeast Asian dining practices. In the more pedestrian curry shops or "banana leaf" restaurants, there will usually be a row of wash basins and soap for customers to clean up. Even with clean hands, diners should touch only the food on their plate, never that in the communal dishes, and the left hand is used to hold the serving spoon to keep it clean.

Chinese food is more likely to be eaten with chopsticks, although at some Chinese food stalls and in many Chinese homes, forks, spoons and knives are used. At a ten-course Chinese meal, chopsticks are *de rigueur*. Sucking or licking the tips of the chopsticks is considered impolite and contact between mouth and the tips of chopsticks is kept minimal. Spoons are set out for larger mouthfuls. In between

mouthfuls, never leave your chopsticks stack into the rice or food—this is associated with rice offered to religious idols and the dead. Always place the chopsticks together resting on a bowl or with the tips on your plate and the handles on the table.

Often before and always at the end of the meal, hot towels are handed round for cleaning the face and hands. It is also common to receive individually wrapped rolls of perfumed, wet paper towels in many Chinese restaurants.

Chinese tea is the traditional drink with Chinese food—the hot, slightly bitter brew of oolong tea is a superb accompaniment to oily stir-fries. If you prefer something milder and sweeter, you can ask for a pot of chrysanthemum tea. Hot water for the pot is always refillable, but the first brew is always the thickest. For some, however, there is nothing quite like beer to take the heat off your tongue and to cool you down when you eat spicy food. One of the major local beers, Tiger, has won awards world-wide and has even been immortalized in Anthony Burgess' satirical novel, *Time for a Tiger*.

ABOVE: Some ancient Chinese traditions live on in modern Singapore, where a teahouse offers a chance for repose while drinking a specially brewed pot of tea.

The Kopitiam Tradition

"Coffee shop talk" is a phrase Singaporeans use to describe gossip, and no wonder since the neighbourhood coffee shop or *kopitiam* is where news, views and grouses are exchanged over a cup of coffee or a quick meal.

In a typical *kopitiam*, a drinks stall at the back is run by the owner, who also sells breakfast items and small snacks. A typical breakfast at a *kopitiam* might include two slices of locally made bread lightly toasted over a charcoal grill, and served with a thick slice of chilled, melting butter, slathered with *kaya* (coconut and egg jam) or sprinkled with sugar. Soft-boiled eggs, eaten with soy sauce and pepper, are another *kopitiam* staple. The other kinds of food come from stall holders, who lease space from the owner. These stall holders are usually of various ethnicities, adding to the customer's variety of choice cuisine. This is in fact where the concept for the food court originated—lots of food stalls with independent owner-cooks sharing the same dining venue. More often than not, there will be a stall selling Malay Nasi Lemak (fragrant rice cooked in coconut milk wrapped in banana leaves), *roti prata* and "economical noodles" (Hokkien *mee* or rice vermicelli stir-fried in sweet soy sauce, served with side dishes)—so named for its extremely reasonable price.

Breakfast is washed down with *kopi-o* (sweet black coffee) or *kopi susu* (coffee with a few dollops of sweetened condensed milk), the usual morning beverages of heartland Singapore. Other variations of the morning brew include *kopi-C*, which is basically coffee with evaporated milk (the 'C' is for Carnation, a brand of evaporated milk). Replace *kopi* with the word *teh*, and you get tea. Add the word *kosong*—which means "empty" in Malay—and you get your cuppa *sans* sugar.

In a decent *kopitiam* of old, the owner roasted and ground his own beans, and some developed quite a reputation for their brew—as did their Malay counterparts in *sarabat* (ginger tea) stalls with their *teh tarik*. Singapore coffee is thick and strong; roasted corn and margarine are often added, along with a dollop of syrupy thick sweetened condensed milk.

The local brew had a reputation of being illegal—stories circulated of how opium, once legal and easily available, was added to boost the potency of caffeine. Now most *kopitiam* owners depend on coffee factories for their supplies.

In the mornings, the *kopitiam* fills up quickly with people having breakfast before heading to the office or school. In the late morning, the crowd thins out but there are always a few shift workers or senior citizens who linger over a cuppa for some "coffee shop talk".

Towards lunch time, children attending the afternoon session drift in for an early lunch before school, followed by those who have just finished the morning session. Part of the lunch crowd is made up of workers from nearby shops and offices. Afternoons are a little quiet until evening brings back people in search of dinner, then the diners give way to those who gather to socialize over a pint of beer or stout.

The ebb and flow of customers depends much on the *kopitiam*'s location and character. Some pack up by early evening, while others only do so in the wee hours of the morning. The *kopitiam*, in spite of rising competition from upmarket air-conditioned food centres and restaurants, firmly remains the heart and soul of Singapore.

ABOVE, CENTRE: This watercolor by Daniel Wegera captures the tranquil mood of the old-style Singapore coffee shop—as much a social centre as a place to eat and drink. ABOVE: These flask-like kettles, ideal for making coffee, are part of the typical *kopitiam* kitchenware. Coffee powder is scooped onto a muslin sieve placed over the opening, and hot boiling water is poured over the powder. The resulting brew is a smoky, fragrant concoction that provides a powerful caffeine jolt.

Chinese Food in Singapore
A potluck of Hokkien, Teochew and Cantonese cuisines

When two Chinese meet, the traditional greeting is to ask whether the other has eaten, highlighting the central place of food in Chinese culture. The greeting must surely have been brought about by the cycles of famine long a part of Chinese history, which have made Chinese cooks firm followers of the adage "waste not, want not". This approach to food is also characteristic of a people with strong roots in the soil; you ate whatever was plentiful, or in season, and you made the best you could of it. And Chinese everywhere, including Singapore, do make the best of everything they can get their hands on.

A little can go a long way when there are several kinds of ingredients cut small, tossed into a hot *kuali* (wok) with a bit of oil, and stir-fried with garlic and fermented soybeans. Slicing food into bite-size pieces makes for rapid, even cooking. Small pieces are also easier to eat when you are manipulating two thin pieces of wood to pick up your food, and they simplify sharing in the communal style of eating. Although large chunks of meat are not unknown, these are cooked until the meat falls away from the bone and can be eaten in bite-sizes, or else the meat is cut into small pieces before being taken to the table. When using large meat cuts to sweeten soups, the meat is often not eaten, but is left in the pot with remaining herbs.

While stir-frying is very Chinese, so is steaming, where the prepared food is placed in bamboo baskets over a *kuali* of boiling water. Equally popular is braising or stewing—the long, slow cooking with seasonings such as soy sauce, bean paste, oyster sauce or garlic transforms tough cuts into melt-in-your-mouth, flavourful morsels. Deep- or stir-frying is sometimes combined with braising or steaming; a sauce prepared with chicken stock, rice wine, soy sauces, perfumed greens like spring onions and coriander leaves (cilantro), and other colourful vegetables, is poured over the deep-fried ingredient.

Many Chinese dishes combine several vegetables with meat or seafood, making for naturally colourful food. Pit-roasting is another cooking technique used for delicacies such as roasted suckling pig, and various roasted meats are done in kiln-like ovens or large drums—note however that Chinese "roast" chicken is actually deep-fried.

Although the basic cooking techniques are used by Chinese everywhere, different provinces tend to prefer certain techniques and ingredients. The northern Chinese use mutton, unheard of in the south, which accounts for the unfamiliarity Singaporean Chinese have with mutton. Northern cooks use more garlic and bean paste, while cooks in Sichuan in the West and Hunan in central China rely on chillies as well. Northerners eat *mantou*, a wheat-flour bread, as a staple, and rice is more common in the south.

Foods from all regions of China are well-represented in Singapore. There is both elegant Shanghainese and Beijing cooking, the stuff of Imperial kitchens, as well as spicy Sichuan and Hunanese food. From the south comes Cantonese cuisine, which can range from elegant nouvelle Hong Kong with its small portions and fruity flavours, to hearty, homely *sa poh* braised food cooked in claypots. Cantonese roast meats such as suckling pig, roast pork and red-roasted pork (*char siew*) are justifiably popular.

Cantonese *dim sum* or "little hearts" go down well the world over and Singapore is no different. *Dim sum* is especially popular for lunch, whether quick or leisurely. In Singapore, the Hokkiens (originally from Fujian Province) are the largest dialect group, followed by the Teochews (from Swatow), then the Cantonese. The relatively small size of the Cantonese community is not obvious given the high profile of Cantonese cuisine in Singapore. Teochew cuisine is also quite popular, and is characterised by light soups, steamed food and fish dishes—many in the community were, and still are, in the seafood business.

Light and very popular not only for breakfast, but lunch, dinner and supper is Teochew savoury porridge, rice gruel eaten with various boiled, stewed, steamed and fried dishes, whether cooked at home or eaten at porridge restaurants.

By contrast, fewer restaurants serve the more homely Hokkien cuisine, with its characteristically hearty braised dishes, such as *tau yew bak* (pork braised in black soy sauce) eaten with steamed buns, oyster omelette and Popiah. The cuisine is strong on pork dishes, especially "white pork" meat with plenty of marbling, trotters complete with the fatty skin, or belly pork. Garlic and soy sauce are used generously. Soups are good, especially heavy soups with meatballs and vegetables.

One much-loved Hokkien contribution to Singapore hawker food is Hokkien *mee*, the yellow noodles found not only in Hokkien Fried Noodles and Hae Mee (*mee* in prawn-flavoured soup), but also in Malay Mee Rebus, Soto Ayam, and Indian Mee Goreng. In fact, much of the character of the food cooked by once-mobile hawkers, now located in food centres, comes from the wide range of ingredients used by different dialect groups, put together in different ways by other communities.

Like yellow Hokkien *mee*, Teochew fishball is a classic ingredient accepted by all the races in Singapore and found in many dishes, be it Indian Rojak, Chinese noodle soup, or cooked with Malay sambal. The fishball is made by grinding fish meat with tapioca flour, salt and water to get a bouncy, white fish paste. The same fish paste can also be used to make fishcake, which is another essential garnish in Singapore food.

Although it may appear that the Chinese live only to eat, they also eat with health in mind. Stalls specialising in tonic or herbal soups are now common in Singapore. These soups, usually a combination of chicken and ginseng or pork with Sichuan vegetables or watercress double-boiled for long periods of time, are believed to nourish the body.

Yet long before the link between food and health became fashionable, the Chinese were developing a complex philosophy of dietetics. Certain foods are believed to be "cooling", or *yin*, while others are "heaty", or *yang,* and some are neutral. The human constitution is classified the same way, with some people being more *yin*, while others are more *yang*. The Chinese believe that a balance of *yin* and *yang* in the body by eating the correct foods maintains good health, and it is therefore important to eat a wide range of foods in moderation.

OPPOSITE: Cantonese cuisine is a perennial favourite, especially the tidbits known as *dim sum*, enjoyed here in a typical Chinatown teahouse cum restaurant. ABOVE: Elegant Chinese restaurants, such as Li Bai, serve impeccable Cantonese cuisine to discerning gourmets.

Malay and Indian Food

On the food trail from Malaysia to Indonesia and the Indian Subcontinent

Both Indian and Malay cuisines are favourites for multi-racial gatherings in Singapore, especially since local Indian and Malay dishes are always *halal* (conforming to Muslim dietary laws). The Mughal Emperors and their court were Muslim, and it has become traditional in India and Indian restaurants the world over not to serve pork, which is prohibited by the Muslims, as well as beef, because of religious strictures imposed by Hinduism, which venerates the cow.

Malay food

Fragrant roots such as galangal (*lengkuas*), ginger and fresh turmeric, together with shallots, garlic, fresh and dried chillies, with emphatic overtones from lemongrass (*serai*) and *belachan* are what distinguish Malay curries from Indian ones. Malay cuisine is the link between Indonesia, to the west and south, and Thailand to the north. Although the results are rather different, there is a certain amount of overlap, especially with the food of nearby Sumatra and, in northern Malaysia, with Thailand. fresh roots and seasonings typical of Malay food are used with spices like coriander, cumin and fennel, although these combinations are common in Indian curries. Coconut milk, widely used throughout tropical Asia, is added liberally to enrich many Malay dishes. Malay food also tends to be slightly sweet with palm or white sugar being a common ingredient, while tamarind juice gives a subtle tangy taste.

Although Malay food is not as prominent in Singapore as Chinese food, it is nonetheless part of the mainstream diet even for Chinese Singaporeans. Familiar favourites are the Malay classics such as Korma, Beef Rendang, Chicken Curry and the various sambals. An indispensible item in Malay cuisine, Sambal Belachan, has become so undeniably a part of the Singaporean diet, it appears as a standard condiment in most Chinese restaurants, complete with half a lime.

Nasi Lemak, a coconut-rich rice dish served with a variety of accompaniments such as crisp fried *ikan bilis* (dried baby anchovies), peanuts, prawn, shredded omelette and Chilli Sambal is what many Singaporeans eat for breakfast. Some of the *kuih* (cakes) associated with the Nonyas were Malay to start with, and, along with Chinese *chui kuih* (steamed rice cakes topped with Preserved Chinese Cabbage) and Indian *roti prata*, are consumed for breakfast and at teatime.

The highlight of Singapore's Malay cuisine is *satay*, thought by some to evolve from the Arab kebab but with a character all its own. *Satay* has spawned two Chinese versions: *satay chelop*, known locally as *lok lok*—bite-sized pieces of meat, vegetables and various items speared onto *satay* sticks and cooked in a bubbling pot of peanut-based gravy—Nonya pork *satay*, and *satay bee hoon*.

On the other hand, *roti john* ("John's bread") was said to have been inspired by a homesick tourist named John who, so the story goes, was in search of a sandwich. A helpful hawker sliced up a French loaf, clapped in a mixture of minced mutton and onion, dipped it in beaten egg, and fried it until crisp. Historically speaking, however, the dish—now a staple at Muslim food stalls—is more likely an adaptation of the Indian Muslim dish, Murtabak (stuffed fried pancake).

Indian food

The Indians, who form just over 7 percent of Singapore's population, are predominantly from the south of the sub-continent (mostly Tamils from Tamil Nadu, and some Malayalees from Kerala in the southwest). Like the Chinese, the Southerners arrived first and came in larger numbers compared to the Sindhis, Gujeratis, Bengalis, Punjabis and other Northerners who came later. Naturally, South Indian cuisine is more established and more common than that of the north.

Even non-Indians can easily tell the more fiery southern food from the milder Northern dishes. Indian cooking calls for spices such as coriander, cardamom, cumin, fennel and cloves, but north and south use them differently. North Indian

OPPOSITE: Delectable Malay food can be enjoyed throughout Singapore in food stalls and restaurants, and even a few fine dining venues. BELOW: Festivals, such as the Muslim Hari Raya, at the end of the fasting month of Ramadan, provide an opportunity for feasting as well as for family reunions. Visitors of all races are welcome during the traditional "open house".

food is enriched with yogurt or cream, with a blend of chopped herbs, fresh chillies, and tomatoes added late in the cooking for a subtle flavour. These thicker curries are eaten with a variety of breads from unleavened flat *chapati* to puffy tandoor-baked *naan*. Singapore's North Indians, like North Indians elsewhere, have a largely wheat-based diet, although they eat at least one meal of rice daily.

South Indians, on the other hand, eat a rice-based diet that suits their more liquid curries, which are often enriched with coconut milk. However, the Southerners have their breads too: fluffy and ghee-rich *roti prata*, and *dosai*, tangy pancakes made from a fermented rice and *dhal* batter. *Dosai* do nicely for breakfast, lunch, tea and dinner, especially when they come in a variety of forms: crisp and paper-thin, fat and fluffy, plain or with curry filling.

The extensive use of dried beans and lentils in a variety of ways from staples to snacks gives Indian food a clout with vegetarians. *Dosai* shops are also often vegetarian restaurants since vegetarianism is mandated by Hinduism.

Named after the "plate" on which the food is served, "banana leaf restaurants" reduce the dishwashing load by having customers eat off banana leaves. Rice is surrounded by your choice of vegetables and *dhal* curries, crisp *pappadam*, cooling yogurt and tangy *rasam* (pepper water). Some banana leaf restaurants cater to carnivores, offering meat and seafood curries, the most popular being the local Fish Head Curry, which originated in Singapore.

While Singapore Indian food has most of the characteristics of Indian food elsewhere, it has not escaped the influences of the other ethnic communities. Apart from Fish Head Curry, another local Indian favourite is Indian Mee Goreng, fried yellow noodles prepared with chillies, potato, bean sprouts, tomato ketchup and some curry spices. There is also Indian Rojak, which has rather non-Indian ingredients, such as Javanese *tempeh*, Chinese fried *tauhu* and fishcake along with boiled potatoes, hard-boiled eggs in batter and a choice of fritters, all eaten dipped in a sweet potato sauce, served with green chilies and slices of onion and cucumber.

Sup Kambing (mutton soup) is another Indian dish with a Chinese accent: lots of fresh coriander leaves (cilantro) to perk up the robust soup seasoned with spices. The soup comes invariably with crusty *roti perancis* (French bread). South Indian food is often prepared by Indian Muslims, some of whose restaurants along North Bridge Road are well-known for their Murtabak and *biryani*, a fragrant saffron-coloured rice flavoured with fried onions, spices, raisins and nuts, cooked with mutton or chicken.

BELOW: Indian Rojak, a distinctive Singapore Indian version of a Malay Indonesian snack, is a dish you'd never find in India. RIGHT: So-called "banana leaf restaurants" offer a selection of food served on the original disposable plate. Typical dishes include the famous Singapore Indian dish, Fish Head Curry, as well as succulent crabs and spicy prawns.

The Best Show in Town
Singapore Street Food, Hawker Style

They once roamed the streets of Singapore, itinerant food hawkers who fed a mostly male populace too busy earning a living to cook for themselves. Today, hawkers no longer ply their trade in the streets, but have been relocated inside permanent food centres which most Singaporeans persist in calling hawker centres.

Today, most women in Singapore work outside the home, and home-cooked meals are therefore something of a weekend event rather than a daily necessity. Most people eat out at least once a day, and the top choice for a quick, tasty meal is the food centre or the increasingly more upmarket food court. Food stalls are now permanent fixtures in a variety of places ranging from an open-air setting to covered markets and food centres, to air-conditioned food courts with more comfort and better decor.

The ubiquitous Chinese noodles were and still are the staples of any good food centre. Take your pick from rice, wheat, mung or soya bean noodles. They come thin, thick, flat, round or square, fresh, dried or fried in oil. You can have your noodles braised, stir-fried, tossed in spicy sauce mixture or dunked in plain or spicy soup. They also come in Chinese, Indian or Malay styles. The choice at a regular food centre now stretches even further, beyond noodles to rice with a variety of Chinese dishes, Malay or Indian curries, barbecued seafood, to hamburgers, hot dogs, steaks and chops, and even pizza!

Eating at a food centre involves all your senses. Your ears are assailed by the shouts of the cooks, the clatter and bang of ladles on giant woks or *kualis*; your nose twitches with every waft of fragrant steam from bubbling pots and *kualis* sitting over roaring fires. It is amazing how experienced hawkers have developed their own unique method to the madness. Using a system of spoons, coins, and even clothes pegs, hawkers have created a reliable way to remember the many different orders and the special requests customers have. A good rapport is necessary to establish a loyal clientele in the face of such fierce competition—and if the hawker remembers his customer's regular order, even before they ask for it, that is one sure way of showing who is boss.

A reputation for good food or a convenient location make some food centres more popular than others, and if you come at peak hours, you may even have to stand over someone having his meal in order to get a table. Some die-hard foodies would not bat an eyelid at the hour-long queues for their favourite hawker dish.

ABOVE: The Singaporean government takes the national pastime very seriously. Some roads, like this junction in Chinatown, are blocked off to traffic in the evenings till early morning, and are dedicated to street-side dining. LEFT: Kreta Ayer Wet Market is famous for its array of fresh market produce and more exotic delights such as turtle meat, frogs and eels.

A food centre is not the place for elegant dining, but the no-frills approach does keep the cost of eating low. You can get a decent meal for under five dollars, a phenomenon common to most Southeast Asian countries. And there are many Singaporeans who will swear that the food at such places beats that dished out in some fancy restaurants. Certainly, the Char Kway Teow (stir-fried rice noodles), Wanton Mee (noodles with pork and prawn dumplings) and Mee Goreng (fried Hokkien *mee* with egg) served up at many five-star hotels are often poor imitations of the real thing to be found in the hot and noisy hawker centres. Some also vow that the food courts, which serve basically the same fare in air-conditioned comfort, but at higher prices, pale in comparison in terms of the quality of the cuisine.

This may be why the Satay Club at Clarke Quay in Singapore continues to be a top draw with both visitors and locals. Here the tables are set under the stars and your friendly satay man grills your sticks of satay nearby. You go home with your hair smelling of grilled meat, but nothing beats this meal of barbecued meat dipped in a spicy peanut sauce eaten in the cool darkness of the night, lit softly by lamps and the glow of coal fires all around. Unlike most other hawker centres with their predominance of Chinese food stalls, the Satay Club is a showcase not only of that Malay pièce de résistance, satay, but also of other Indian and Malay street food. The Satay Club is rare in still

having the same open-air ambience that it has had for decades, even if it is on a larger, more varied scale.

The drink evolution

Drinks in food centres in Singapore go beyond the prosaic to the delicious, with plain-looking soybean milk, downright exotic black grass herb jelly, freshly squeezed sugar cane juice and healthy fruit juices blended on the spot. Familiar cow's milk becomes *susu bandung*, milk flavoured with rose syrup and coloured a garish pink. At a typical dessert stall, there are plastic containers filled with "red rubies" (water chestnut bits covered in tapioca flour), green jelly-like *chendol* strips made of glutinous rice flour, almond-flavoured jelly and grass jelly cubes, sitting in a custom-made tray. Many Singapore desserts are eaten with shaved ice, the most popular being Ice Kachang: coconut jelly, crunchy seaweed gelatine, *atap* seeds, mashed strawberries and other fillings topped with a mountain of ice shavings, doused generously with evaporated milk, red and green coloured syrup and palm sugar—the perfect way to round off a Singapore feast.

BELOW: Ordering and enjoying a Chinese meal, or any other type of food in Singapore, is easy, especially with menus in English and prices clearly stated. Photographs of the dishes are usually displayed on the menus—this is especially helpful when ordering dishes with curious names!

The Singapore Kitchen
All modern appliances gratefully accepted

At first glance, the typical Singapore kitchen is like its counterpart in any Western country: modern, with tiled floors, electrical appliances and the refrigerator so essential in a tropical climate. Look a little closer, however, and you'll find a number of subtle differences. Not all kitchens, for example, have ranges complete with an oven, as most cooking is done on the top of a stove. Electric toaster ovens used for grilling and toasting are, however, increasingly making their way into Singapore kitchens. Gas is preferred for simmering, frying and steaming, as the heat can be quickly adjusted. It is worth noting that very high heat is required for stir-frying Chinese dishes and for heating oil for deep-frying. Most

stove tops, whether Italian or German brands come with a double- or triple-ring burner for this purpose.

Almost every Singapore kitchen has an **electric rice cooker**, which guarantees soft, fluffy rice consistently and keeps it warm for latecomers. Although not essential, you'll find it a great help if you eat rice fairly often.

Saucepans are normally of enamel or stainless steel; aluminium is best avoided, especially for dishes containing tamarind or other acidic ingredients. Traditional cooks still insist on Chinese **claypots** or unglazed earthenware pots (often known by their Malay name, *belanga*), for certain dishes. These are generally inexpensive as well as attractive, and often available in Asian specialty shops overseas.

Essential for all types of Singaporean food, the conical **wok** is known locally by its Chinese name, *kuali*. The wok has got to be the best designed, multi-purpose kitchen utensil anywhere. When food is tossed about during stir-frying, the sloping sides ensure that the food falls back into the wok and not outside, and less oil is required for deep-frying. For dishes requiring a considerable reduction of the sauce, the wide wok allows the correct amount of evaporation. If you use an electric burner rather than gas fire, try to find a flat-bottomed wok. Always choose the heaviest wok you can find; cast iron, once the preferred material, is increasingly being replaced by various alloys.

Various types of steamers are available, but even here, the wok holds its own. With the addition of a perforated metal disc that sits about two-thirds of the way up inside the wok, the wok becomes a fuss-free steamer. Just boil water in the wok, place the food on plates, and on the disc, then cover the wok with a large domed lid. A woven **bamboo steaming basket**, aesthetically appealing as well as practical, is

designed to be set inside a wok; the bamboo absorbs moisture as the steam rises, preventing it from falling back onto the food. If using a metal steamer, put a folded towel under the lid to absorb moisture.

Singapore's Indian kitchens have traditionally used a heavy **iron griddle** or *tawa* for cooking *chapati*, *dosai* and other breads, although some modern cooks prefer to use a large nonstick frying pan for such tasks.

A flat frying spatula is used for stir-frying in a wok, while wire-mesh baskets, traditionally made of brass with a bamboo handle, are ideal for lifting deep-fried food out of the wok, or for removing noodles from boiling water.

A large, heavy wooden chopping board partnered by a strong cleaver with a blade about $7^1/_2$–10 cm (3–4 inches) deep are indispensable for cutting up poultry, crab and fish, for chopping vegetables and for mincing fish or meat to the desired sizes. Most Singapore cooks keep a granite **mortar and pestle** on hand for quick pounding of small amounts of various spices and seasonings. While acknowledging that this age-old method achieves a better result, most modern cooks prefer the speed and ease of an electric blender for grinding dried spices as well as large amounts of seasonings for the spice paste (*rempah*) that forms the basis of many dishes.

Preparing a spice paste

Whether you are using a mortar and pestle or a blender or food processor to prepare the *rempah* used in many Singaporean dishes, you should always follow certain rules. All ingredients should be peeled and sliced first. The hardest ingredients (such as galangal and lemongrass) should be processed until fine before adding softer ingredients like shallots, chilies and ginger. *Belachan* should be added at the last moment and processed just to mix well. Dried spices should be ground separately from the spices mentioned above. While you are blending the spices, you may need to add a little liquid to keep the blades turning. If the *rempah* is to be fried, add a one or two spoonfuls of cooking oil, and coconut milk or stock, as in the recipe.

OPPOSITE AND ABOVE: East truly meets West in a Singapore kitchen, where the Asian wok and Southeast Asian condiments and ingredients meet modern and time-saving devices like microwave ovens, rice cookers and blenders.

Authentic Singapore Ingredients

Agar-agar is a form of gelatine made from seaweed that sets without refrigeration. It is used to make many Asian desserts and is sold in long strands or as a powder in a small packet. Use 1 teaspoon of the powder to set 1–1$\frac{1}{2}$ cups (250–375 ml) of liquid. Instant jelly powder is similar to agar-agar but is softer; agar-agar sets a bit harder.

Banana leaves infuse a delicate flavour and aroma to food. They are often used as wrappers when steaming or grilling dishes, or as little trays to hold food when cooking. Soften the leaves slightly in boiling water for about 10 seconds before use to prevent them from cracking and tearing when wrapping foods

Bangkuang is a root vegetable native to tropical America, where it is known as jicama. It has a crunchy white flesh and beige skin that peels off quite easily. It is excellent eaten raw with a spicy dip or cooked until soft like the filling in Popiah (page 52). Substitute daikon radish.

Belachan or dried prawn paste is a dense mixture of fermented ground prawns with a remarkably strong odour

It is sold in dried blocks that range in colour from caramel to dark brown. It should be roasted before use—either wrapped in foil and dry-roasted in a wok or skillet, or toasted over a gas flame on the end of a fork or back of a spoon—to enhance its flavour and kill bacteria. In some recipes, *belachan* is ground with the rest of the ingredients in a mortar or blender and then fried in oil without toasting. It is not to be confused with fermented prawn sauce (*hay koh*) which tastes and smells different—see below.

Black bean paste (*tau cheo*) is similar to Japanese miso but much saltier—made of soft, slightly fermented soybeans in a salty brown sauce with a distinctive tang. They are usually mashed and used to season fish, noodle and some vegetable dishes. Sold in jars in supermarkets, the basic black bean paste contains only soybeans, water and salt. Sweetened versions, or those with added chilli and garlic are also available. Miso makes a good substitute, but as it is less salty than black bean paste, you will need to add some salt.

Bok choy is a crunchy, leafy green vegetable that is widely used in Chinese cuisine. A large vegetable with plump white stalks and dark green leaves, fresh *bok choy* is available all year round in fresh markets and supermarkets. Store *bok choy* refrigerated in a plastic bag for no more than 2 days.

Bottled chilli sauce in Singapore comes in many different varieties. Most of them are quite sweet, having the consistency of tomato ketchup, with a blend of ingredients that generally includes chillies, garlic, vinegar, sugar, salt, onions and tomatoes. Western hot sauces like Tabasco do not make good substitutes as they are sour rather than sweet. Look for any type of bottled Asian chilli sauce that is bright red and quite sweet.

Brown mustard seeds are small, round seeds used in many southern Indian cuisines. They impart an almost nutty flavour to dishes. Do not substitute with yellow mustard seeds as the flavour is different.

Candlenuts are waxy, cream-coloured nuts similar in size and texture to macadamia nuts, which can be used as a substitute, although less-expensive almonds or cashews will also do. They are never eaten raw or on their own, but are chopped, ground and cooked with other seasonings. They are added to Malay and Nonya curries and spice mixes for flavour and texture. They go rancid quickly because of their high oil content, so buy in small quantities and keep them refrigerated.

Cardamom pods are used to flavour curries and desserts—giving foods a heady, sweet scent. The fibrous, straw-coloured pods enclose 15–20 pungent, black seeds. The pods should be bruised lightly with a cleaver or a pestle when used whole. Do not substitute ground cardamom as it is virtually flavourless compared to the pods.

Dried chillies

Fresh red chillies

Bird's-eye chillies

Chillies are indispensable in Asian cooking. The commonly-used fresh green and red Asian **finger-length chillies** are moderately hot. Tiny red, green or yellow-orange *chili padi* or bird's-eye chillies are very hot, designed for strong palates. **Dried chillies** are usually cut into lengths and soaked in warm water to soften before use. Dried chillies have a very different flavour from fresh ones. To reduce the heat, discard some or all of the chilli seeds before preparation as part of a spice mix.

Chilli powder, a crucial ingredient in Indian cooking, is a hot seasoning made from ground dried chillies. It is not the same as Mexican chilli powder which contains a mix of paprika, cumin, thyme and other spices. Western paprika is also relatively milder and tastes completely different from Asian chilli powder.

Chinese or **Napa cabbage** has tightly packed white stems and pale green leaves. It has a mild, delicate taste and should only be cooked for a few minutes to retain its colour and crunchy texture. Chinese cabbage is a good source of calcium, potassium and iron, and is often eaten in soups. Available year round in supermarkets.

Chinese celery is often referred to in Singapore as "local" celery. The stems are very slender and more fragrant than normal celery—more of a herb than a vegetable. The leaves are generously used to garnish a variety of Chinese dishes. Substitute celery leaves or Italian parsley.

Chye sim is a leafy green vegetable with slightly crunchy stems. Available in supermarkets in Asia, *chye sim* is now increasingly available in Western countries too. Substitute any other leafy greens.

Coconut milk or **cream** are used in many dishes in Singapore in much the same way that milk or cream are used in Western cooking. They are made by squeezing the flesh of freshly grated mature coconuts. To obtain **coconut cream**, about ¹/₂ cup (125 ml) water is added for each grated coconut, then squeezed and strained. **Thick coconut milk** is obtained by adding 1 cup (250 ml) of water to the grated coconut, then pressing it to extract the juice. **Thin coconut milk** is obtained by adding another 2 cups (500 ml) of water to the already squeezed grated coconut and pressing it a second

time. Although freshly pressed cream and milk have more flavour, they are now widely sold canned and in packets which are quick, convenient and quite tasty. Canned or packet coconut cream or milk comes in varying consistencies depending on the brand, and you will need to try them out and adjust the thickness by adding water as needed. In general, you should add 1 cup (250 ml) water to 1 cup (250 ml) canned or packet coconut cream to obtain thick coconut milk, and 2 cups (500 ml) water to 1 cup (250 ml) coconut cream to obtain thin coconut milk. These mixing ratios are only general guides and you should adjust the consistency to individual taste.

Coriander is a pungent spice plant that is essential in Southeast Asian cooking. It is widely available and can easily be grown at home. **Coriander leaves** (also known as cilantro) are used as a herb and a garnish. They are sold in bunches, sometimes with the roots still attached. Small, round **coriander seeds** have a mild citrus fragrance. They are used whole or ground into a powder that is the basis for many curries and sauces.

Cumin seeds (*jintan putih*) are pale brown to black in colour and ridged on the outside. They impart an earthy flavour and are used whole, or roasted and then ground to a fine powder. Cumin seeds are usually partnered with coriander seeds in basic spice mixes, and are often dry-roasted or fried in oil to intensify their flavour.

Curry leaves are the tiny, slender leaves of the curry leaf shrub. They do not taste like curry but are so-named because of their frequent use in Indian curries. They are sold in sprigs of 8–15 small, slightly pointed, green leaves with a distinct fragrance often associated with Indian curries. There is no substitute for curry leaves.

Curry powder is a commercial spice blend that generally includes cumin seeds, coriander seeds, turmeric, ginger, cinnamon and cloves. Different combinations vary in colour and flavour and are used for different types of curries—meat, fish or chicken. Use an all-purpose blend if a specific curry powder is not available.

Daikon radishes are large root vegetables also known as "white carrots" in Singapore. They are juicy but bland, unlike the smaller western radish. They can grow to a length of 40 cm (15 in) or more. Choose firm and heavy daikons without any bruises on them. Scrub or peel the skin before you grate or slice the flesh.

Dried black Chinese mushrooms should be soaked in warm water for 20

minutes before use. The tough stems are usually discarded and only the caps are eaten. These mushrooms vary in thickness and quality. Try to buy the thickest ones for dishes that feature mushrooms as a main ingredient.

Dried Chinese sausages (lap cheong) are sweet, reddish sausages delicately perfumed with rice wine. They are used as an ingredient in stir-fries or braised dishes rather than being eaten on their own like European sausages. Sold in pairs, they keep almost indefinitely without refrigeration.

Dried prawns (hay bee) are a popular Asian ingredient used in sauces and sambals. They are tiny, orange-coloured sun-dried saltwater prawns. They keep for several months and should be soaked in water for 5 minutes to soften slightly before use. Dried prawns come in various sizes and the very small ones have the heads and tails attached. Look for dried prawns that are pink and plump and avoid any grayish ones. Better quality dried prawns are bright orange in colour and shelled.

Dried salted fish is used as a seasoning or condiment in Asia. It is not necessary to soak in water before use, just slice and fry until crisp.

Eggplants used in Singapore are generally of the slender, purple-skinned variety, 15–20 cm (6–8 in) long. They are mild and need not be salted before use

Fennel seeds look like cumin seeds, but are larger and paler. They add a sweet fragrance to a number of Malay and Indian dishes, with a flavour similar to liquorice or anise. The seeds are used whole or ground.

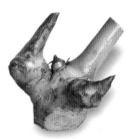

Fenugreek seeds are flat and slightly rectangular, about 3 mm ($1/_8$ in) across, light brown in colour, with a deep furrow along their lengths. They are bitter, so use sparingly.

Five spice powder is a blend of ground dried spices containing cinnamon, cloves, fennel, Sichuan pepper and ginger. It is sold in small packets in the spice section in most supermarkets.

Galangal (lengkuas) is a fragrant root from the ginger family. It imparts a

distinctive flavour to many Southeast Asian dishes. Try to find young, pinkish galangal as it is more tender. Peel and slice the fresh root before grinding as it is quite tough. Galangal is also available dried, frozen or packed in water, but always try to get fresh galangal root whenever possible as it is more fragrant.

Garlic chives (*koo chye*) or Chinese chives have flattened leaves that resemble thin spring onions. They have a strong garlicky flavour and are often added to noodle or stir-fried vegetable dishes during the final stages of cooking.

Ghee is rich clarified butter oil with all the milk solids removed. Widely used in Indian cooking, it can be heated to high temperatures without burning. Although ghee is very high in cholesterol, it adds a rich and delicious flavour to foods. Available in cans in supermarkets and Indian provision shops. Butter or vegetable oil make good substitutes.

Hay koh (fermented prawn sauce) is a black, pungent, molasses-like seasoning made of fermented prawns, salt, sugar and thickeners. It is used as a sauce or a dip. It is sometimes labelled as *petis* and is unrelated to *belachan*.

Kaffir limes (*limau purut*), also known as fragrant limes, are about the same size as normal limes but with a very knobbly and intensely fragrant skin, but virtually no juice. **Kaffir lime leaves** (*daun limau purut*) add an intense fragrance to soups and cur-

ries of Malay and Nonya origin. The leaves are added whole to curries, or finely shredded and added to salads, giving them a wonderfully tangy flavour. Kaffir lime leaves are commonly used in Indonesian and Thai cooking, and are available frozen or dried in supermarkets. Frozen leaves are more flavourful than dried ones.

Kailan (kale or Chinese broccoli) is enjoyed for its firm texture and emphatic flavour. Only the tender portions of the stems and young inner leaves are generally eaten, as the outer leaves are quite bitter. The thicker stems are generally peeled and halved lengthwise before cooking. Broccoli stems make a good substitute. Baby *kailan* is a recently developed vegetable grown by crowding the plants together and force-feeding them. They have a crunchy texture and are usually cooked whole.

Fresh yellow wheat noodles
(Hokkien *mee*)

Fresh flat rice noodles
(*kway teow*)

Fresh laksa noodles
(Rice noodles)

Dried rice vermicelli
(*beehoon*)

Dried glass noodles
(*tanghoon*)

Noodles are a universal favourite in Singapore which the Malays, Nonyas and Indians have enthusiastically adopted from the Chinese. Both fresh and dried noodles made from either wheat, rice or mung bean flour are found. **Fresh yellow wheat noodles** (Hokkien *mee*) are heavy, spaghetti-like noodles made from wheat flour and egg. Substitute dried ramen or spaghetti. **Fresh flat rice noodles** (*kway teow*) are ribbon-like noodles about 1 cm ($1/_2$ in) wide, used in soups or fried. Substitute dried rice stick noodles. **Fresh laksa noodles** are round like white spaghetti, but are made from rice flour and traditionally served in laksa soups. Substitute spaghetti. **Dried rice vermicelli** (*beehoon*) are very fine rice threads that must be plunged into boiling water to soften before use. **Dried glass noodles**, made from mung beans, are fine white strands that are generally used in soups. They are also called "cellophane" or "transparent" noodles, both accurate descriptions of their appearance after soaking. Both fresh and dried noodles should be blanched in boiling water before cooking to rinse and revive them—use a pair of long chopsticks to keep them from sticking together.

Kangkung is a nutritious, leafy vegetable also known as morning glory, water convolvulus or water spinach. The leaves and tender tips are often stir-fried. *Bok choy* or spinach make good substitutes.

Laksa leaves, also called *daun kesum*, polygonum or Vietnamese mint, are traditionally added to spicy laksa soup dishes (page 34). The spear-shaped leaves wilt quickly once they are plucked from the stem. They have an intense fragrance reminiscent of lemon with a hint of eucalyptus. There is no real substitute, but a mixture of spearmint and coriander leaves or basil does approximate its flavour and fragrance.

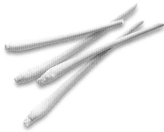

Lemongrass is a fragrant lemony stalk that is either bruised and used whole in soups or curries, or sliced and ground as part of a basic spice mix. It is usually sold in bunches of 3–4 stems in the supermarket. The tough outer layers should be peeled away and only the thick lower third of the stem is used. Always slice the stems before grinding to get a smooth paste.

Limes are essential in Asian cooking. Small limes (*limau kasturi* or kalamansi limes), about the size of a walnut, have a mild and fragrant juice. They are squeezed over noodle dishes and into the ubiquitous Sambal Belachan (page 30). Large limes, with a greenish-yellow skin, have a tart flavour similar to lemons, which may be used as a substitute. Kaffir limes are generally used in dishes of Malay or Nonya origin (see above).

Okra, known locally as ladies' fingers, is usually partnered with eggplant in Indian fish curries. The vegetable has green, curved ridges and ranges from 7–20 cm (3–8 in) in length. It contains edible white seeds and a sticky juice used for thickening some dishes.

Oyster sauce is the rich, thick and dark extract of dried oysters. It is frequently added to stir-fried vegetable and meat dishes, and must be refrigerated once the bottle is opened. Expensive versions made with abalone and vegetarian versions made from mushrooms are also available. Check the ingredients listed on the bottle as many brands are loaded with MSG.

Palm sugar (*gula melaka*) is sold as a solid block or cylinder and is made from the sap of the coconut or *arenga* palm. It varies in colour from gold to light brown and has a faint caramel taste. It should be shaved or grated into small chunks or melted in a microwave oven before using. Substitute brown sugar or maple syrup.

Pandanus leaves impart a subtle fragrance and colour to a range of Malay and Nonya dishes. They are usually tied in a knot and then added to a liquid recipe. Bottled pandanus essence can be substituted in desserts, but if fresh or dried pandanus leaves are not available, omit them from savoury dishes. Vanilla essence may be substituted in dessert recipes.

Plum sauce is a sweet Chinese sauce made from plums, vinegar and sugar. Sold in jars or cans in Chinese stores.

Regular soy sauce   Black soy sauce   Sweet black sauce

Soy sauce is brewed from soybeans and sometimes wheat fermented with salt. It is salty and used as a table dip and cooking seasoning. Black soy sauce is denser, less salty and adds a smoky flavour to dishes. Sweet black sauce is a thick, fragrant sauce used in marinades and sauces.

Pickled mustard cabbage (*kiam chye*) is used in some Chinese and Nonya dishes. Soak the heavily salted cabbage in water for 15 minutes to remove some of the saltiness, repeating if necessary.

Rice flour is made from ground uncooked rice grains. It is used to make the dough or batter for many desserts. Fresh rice flour was traditionally made by soaking rice overnight and then slowly grinding it in a stone mill. The same result may be achieved by grinding soaked rice in a blender. Rice flour is sold in powdered form in packets in supermarkets and Asian speciality shops.

Rice wine is added to some marinades and stir-fried dishes in very much the same way that sherry is used in Western cooking. Substitute Japanese sake or dry sherry.

Sesame oil is extracted from roasted (darker oil) or raw (lighter oil) sesame seeds. It is added to Chinese dishes in small quantities as a final touch for its strong nutty flavour and delicate fragrance. It is never used on its own as a frying medium as high heat turns it bitter.

Firm tofu	Pressed tofu	Deep-fried tofu

Tofu is rich in protein and amazingly versatile. Various types of tofu, originally introduced by the Chinese, are now used by almost every ethnic group in Singapore. **Firm tofu** holds its shape well when cut or cooked and has a strong, slightly sour taste. **Pressed tofu** (often confusingly labelled as firm tofu) has much of the moisture extracted and is therefore much firmer in texture and excellent for stir-fries. Refrigerate fresh tofu immersed in water. Slices of **deep-fried tofu** (*tau foo pok*) are sold ready-made in supermarkets and wet markets, and may be sliced or cubed and added to stir-fried dishes and soups.

Tamarind pulp (*asam*) is the fruit contained in the tamarind tree seed pod. It is sold dried in packets or jars and generally still has some seeds and pod fibres mixed in with the dried pulp. It is used as a souring agent in many dishes. To obtain **tamarind juice**, mash the pulp in warm water, strain and discard any seeds or fibres. If using already cleaned tamarind pulp, slightly reduce the amounts called for in the recipes. The dried pulp keeps indefinitely in an airtight container.

and stains everything permanently, so scrub your knife blade, hands and chopping board immediately after handling. Purchase fresh turmeric root as needed as the flavour fades after a few days. Substitute 1 teaspoon ground turmeric for $2^{1}/_{2}$ cm (1 in) of the fresh root.

White vinegar or Chinese rice vinegar are most commonly used in Singapore cooking. Some recipes call for Chinese black vinegar or red vinegar, both of which have distinctive flavours and are not interchangeable. Balsamic vinegar may be used as a substitute.

Star anise is an eight-pointed dried pod encasing shiny black seeds that have a strong aniseed flavour. The whole spice is usually used when cooking and is discarded before serving. Whole star anise keeps for a year in an airtight container.

Turmeric (*kunyit*) is a root similar to ginger but with a bright yellow flesh and a more pungent flavour. Turmeric has antiseptic and astringent qualities

Wild ginger buds (*bunga kantan*) are the pink buds of the wild ginger plant, also known as torch ginger. They are highly aromatic and lend a distinct fragrance to dishes of Malay and Nonya origin. Available in Asian markets.

Authentic Singapore Recipes

Portions

In homes and restaurants in Singapore, several dishes are presented together on the table family style, allowing diners to help themselves to whatever they want. Small amounts of these dishes are eaten with lots of fragrant fluffy rice or noodles. This makes it difficult to estimate the exact number of portions each recipe will provide. As a general rule, however, the recipes in this book will serve 4 to 6 people as part of a meal with rice and 3 to 4 other main dishes.

Singaporean seasonings

Singaporeans are very fond of strong flavours—spicy, salty, sweet, sour and bitter. The amounts of chilli, soy sauce and sugar given in the following recipes are guides, not absolute measures. Bear in mind that you can always increase the amount of seasonings when preparing a dish. Seasonings at the table may be added later, so be careful not to overdo it in the initial stages.

Sambals, Achars and Condiments

Recipes on pages 29–31 can be prepared in large quantities and stored in a covered glass jar in a refrigerator for a month or in a freezer for 3–4 months. No Singaporean meal is complete without a small bowl of one of these on the dining table.

Ingredients

Many ingredients used in Singaporean have made their way into supermarkets around the world—including coriander leaves (cilantro), coconut milk and lemongrass. Other ingredients like palm sugar, banana leaves, *belachan* and pandanus leaves are less common and need to be sourced from shops specialising in Asian foods. If you're not in Singapore or Malaysia, look for ingredients that are more difficult to find in Asian specialty shops. If they are still difficult to locate, see pages 22–27 for possible substitutes.

Tips on grinding spices

When using a mortar and pestle or blender to prepare spice pastes, it helps to peel and slice all the ingredients before grinding. Grind tougher or drier ingredients first before grinding the softer or wetter ones. Add a little liquid (oil, coconut milk or water, depending on the recipe) to keep the blades turning. Be sure not to overload the blender—if the quantity is large, pulse them in batches and grind each batch before grinding the next. If you have to roast some ingredients before grinding, usually the case with *belachan* (dried prawn paste), allow them to cool down before grinding. Spice pastes need only be ground coarsely—not to a purée. Store unused spice pastes in plastic wrap or an airtight container in the refrigerator or freezer.

Time estimates

Estimates are given for food preparation and cooking, and are based on the assumption that a food processor or blender is used to grind spices.

Sambals, Achars and Condiments

Dried Prawn Sambal

This sambal makes a great snack on bread, and also goes well with stir-fried vegetables and rice.

$1/_2$ cup (125 ml) oil
$1/_2$ teaspoon salt
1 teaspoon sugar

Spice Paste
$3/_4$ cup (100 g) dried prawns, soaked to soften, then drained
15 dried chillies, deseeded, cut into lengths, soaked to soften, drained
20 red finger-length chillies, deseeded and sliced
8 shallots, peeled
6 cloves garlic, peeled
1 tablespoon *belachan* (dried prawn paste)

1 To make the Spice Paste, grind the ingredients in a mortar or blender, adding a little oil if necessary to keep the blades turning.
2 Heat the oil in a skillet and gently stir-fry the Spice Paste over low to medium heat for 10 minutes until fragrant. Season with the salt and sugar, and set aside to cool. The sambal keeps in the refrigerator for up to a week. Skim off excess oil before serving. Just before serving, add a splash of fresh lime juice and serve in a small bowl with rice and barbecued foods.

Makes $1^1/_2$ cups (375 ml)
Preparation time: 20 mins
Cooking time: 15 mins

Sambal Belachan
Prawn Paste Chilli Sauce

This much-loved sambal can be served with almost any meal.

10 red finger-length chillies, deseeded and sliced
2 tablespoons *belachan* (dried prawn paste), toasted (page 22)
3 tablespoons fresh lime juice
1 teaspoon sugar
$^1/_2$ teaspoon salt

Grind all the ingredients in a mortar or blender to make a coarse paste. Keeps in the refrigerator for about 1 week.

Makes $^3/_4$ cup (185 ml)
Preparation time: 10 mins

Flour Crisps

3 shallots, peeled
2 cloves garlic, peeled
$^1/_2$ cup (75 g) plain flour
2 teaspoons butter
$^1/_2$ teaspoon oil
$^1/_2$ teaspoon salt
1 egg
Oil for deep-frying

1 Grind the shallots and garlic in a mortar or blender. Knead this paste with all the other ingredients, except the oil for deep-frying, to form a smooth dough. On a floured surface, roll the dough out as thinly as possible and cut into small squares.
2 Deep-fry the dough squares in very hot oil in a wok until light golden brown and crispy, about 2 to 3 minutes. Set aside to cool. When cooled, store the crisps in an airtight container. Serve as a crunchy topping in Yu Sheng (page 76).

Makes 2 cups
Preparation time: 10 mins
Cooking time: 20 mins

Satay Sauce

4 tablespoons oil
$^1/_2$ cup (75 g) roasted peanuts, skins discarded and coarsely ground
$^1/_2$ tablespoon tamarind pulp, mashed in 2 tablespoons water, squeezed and strained to obtain juice
$^1/_2$ cup (125 ml) water
$^1/_4$ teaspoon salt
1 tablespoon sugar

Spice Paste
1 tablespoon coriander seeds
$^1/_2$ teaspoon cumin seeds
2 stalks lemongrass, thick bottom third only, outer layers removed, inner part sliced
$1^1/_2$ cm ($^3/_4$ in) fresh galangal root, peeled and sliced
4 dried chillies, cut into lengths and soaked in warm water
3 cloves garlic, peeled
2 shallots, peeled

1 Grind the Spice Paste ingredients in a mortar or blender, adding a little oil if necessary to keep the blades turning.
2 Heat the oil in a saucepan over medium to high heat and stir-fry the Spice Paste for 3 to 5 minutes until fragrant. Add the peanuts, tamarind juice and water, and season with salt and sugar. Reduce the heat to low and cook for another 3 minutes, stirring constantly, then remove from the heat. Transfer the sauce to a bowl and serve warm or at room temperature.

Substitute $^1/_2$ cup (6 heaping tablespoons) crunchy peanut butter for the crushed peanuts. Add the peanut butter to the sauce in step 2 and mix thoroughly, then remove from the heat. Satay Sauce can be made in large quantities and kept in the the refrigerator for 2–3 weeks or frozen for 3 months.

Makes 1 cup
Preparation time: 25 mins
Cooking time: 10 mins

Pineapple Satay Sauce

2 candlenuts, roughly chopped
$^1/_2$ stalk lemongrass, thick bottom third only, outer layers removed, inner part sliced
4 dried chillies, cut into lengths, deseeded and soaked to soften
4 shallots, peeled
1 clove garlic, peeled
1 tablespoon oil
$^1/_2$ cup (125 ml) thick coconut milk or $^1/_4$ cup (60 ml) coconut cream mixed with $^1/_4$ cup (60 ml) water
$^1/_2$ tablespoon tamarind pulp mashed in 2 tablespoons water, squeezed and strained to obtain juice
$^1/_2$ cup (75 g) coarsely ground roasted peanuts or 6 heaped tablespoons chunky peanut butter
$^1/_2$ teaspoon palm sugar or brown sugar
$^1/_4$ teaspoon salt
$^1/_4$ cup (50 g) canned or fresh crushed pineapple

1 Grind the candlenuts, lemongrass, chillies, shallots and garlic in a mortar or blender, adding a little oil if necessary to keep the blades turning.
2 Heat the oil in a wok and stir-fry the ground ingredients over medium heat for 5 minutes until fragrant. Add the coconut milk and gently bring to a boil.
3 Reduce the heat, add the tamarind juice and peanuts or peanut butter, and season with the sugar and salt. Simmer gently, stirring constantly, for 2 minutes.
4 Remove from the heat and set aside to cool. When cooled, add the crushed pineapple, mix well and set aside.

Makes $1^1/_2$ cups
Preparation time: 25 mins
Cooking time: 10 mins

Achar Kuning

Pickled Vegetables with Turmeric

$^1/_2$ cup (50 g) peeled and thinly sliced carrot
$^1/_2$ cup (40 g) peeled, deseeded and thinly sliced cucumber
$^1/_2$ cup (80 g) peeled and thinly sliced daikon radish
2 tablespoons coarse salt
1 cm ($^1/_2$ in) fresh turmeric root, sliced, or $^1/_2$ teaspoon ground turmeric
3 slices fresh peeled ginger
2 cloves garlic, peeled
2 tablespoons oil
4 cloves garlic, peeled and left whole
4 shallots, peeled and left whole
1 stalk lemongrass, thick bottom third only, outer layers removed, inner part bruised
2 green *chili padi* (bird's-eye chillies), whole, or 2 red finger-length chillies, deseeded and halved lengthwise
$^1/_4$ teaspoon ground white pepper
1 tablespoon sugar
2 tablespoons white vinegar diluted with 4 tablespoons water

1 Sprinkle the carrot, cucumber and radish with the salt. Cover with a plate and weigh down with a heavy bowl. Set aside for 20 minutes.
2 Grind the turmeric, ginger and garlic to a paste in a mortar or blender, adding a little oil if necessary to keep the blades turning.
3 Rinse the vegetables, drain and squeeze out as much moisture as possible.
4 Heat the oil in a wok over medium heat, add the whole garlic and stir-fry for a minute. Remove and set aside. Then add the shallots and stir-fry for another minute. Remove and set aside.
5 Reduce the heat to low, add the ground paste, lemongrass and *chili padi*, and stir-fry for 5 minutes. Add the vegetables, reserved garlic and shallots, and season with the pepper and sugar. Stir-fry until the sugar dissolves, about 1 minute.
6 Add the diluted vinegar and bring to a boil. Immediately remove from the heat and set aside to cool. This *achar* is best kept in the refrigerator for a day or two to cure before serving. If kept in a sealed jar in the refrigerator, it will keep for up to a month. Serve in a small bowl as a side dish with rice-based meals.

Makes 2 cups
Preparation time: 25 mins
Cooking time: 10 mins

Chilli Ginger Sauce

10 red finger-length chillies, deseeded and sliced
10 cloves garlic, peeled
10 slices ginger (about 30 g/1 oz)
1 tablespoon white vinegar
3–4 tablespoons fresh lemon juice
$1^1/_4$ tablespoons sugar
$^1/_2$ teaspoon salt

Grind all the ingredients coarsely in a mortar or blender. Store, covered, in the refrigerator for up to 1 week. Serve with noodles or Chinese dishes.

Makes 1 cup (250 ml)
Preparation time: 15 mins

Crispy Fried Shallots or Garlic

30 shallots or 30 cloves garlic
$^1/_2$ cup (125 ml) oil

1 Peel and thinly slice the shallots or garlic. Then pat dry with paper towels.
2 Heat the oil in a wok and gently stir-fry the shallots or garlic over medium heat until light golden brown and crisp, about 5 to 7 minutes. Do not allow them to burn or they will taste bitter. Drain, cool completely and store in an airtight container. Reserve the **Shallot** or **Garlic Oil** for frying or seasoning other dishes.

Makes 1 cup
Preparation time: 5 mins
Cooking time: 10 mins

Lontong   Steamed Rice Roll

2 pieces banana leaf about 25 x 20 cm (10 x 8 in), soaked in boiling water for a few seconds,
or 1 piece cheesecloth about 60 x 60 cm (24 x 24 in)
1 cup (200 g) uncooked long-grain rice, soaked in cold water for 15 minutes

1 To make the Lontong, first soften the banana leaves by scalding them in boiling water in a tub or pot for 10 seconds. Drain the leaves and shake dry. Then place one banana leaf over the other and roll into a cylinder 5 cm (2 in) in diameter. Fold one end over and seal with a toothpick. Spoon the rice into the roll and fold the open end of the leaf over and secure with a toothpick; leave two-thirds of the roll empty for the rice to expand during cooking. Place the roll in a pot of boiling water, cover and simmer very gently for 30 minutes. Then remove from the pot and cool to room temperature before serving.
2 If using a cheesecloth instead of banana leaves, fold the cloth in half, place the rice on the cloth and roll it up. Seal one end with a kitchen string, then seal the other end of the cloth with another piece of kitchen string, leaving enough room in the cloth to hold 2 times the amount of uncooked rice. Then proceed to cook as described above.

Makes 2 cups
Preparation time: 20 mins
Cooking time: 30 mins

Classic Hainanese Chicken Rice

The classic Singapore dish made with fresh chicken to achieve a perfect combination of flavours and textures, accompanied by fluffy rice cooked in chicken stock, soup and 3 types of sauces.

8 cups (2 litres) chicken stock or 4 teaspoons chicken stock granules dissolved in 8 cups (2 litres) hot water
1 large fresh chicken (about $1^1/_2$ kg/3 lbs), cleaned and patted dry
1 teaspoon soy sauce
$1/_4$ teaspoon sesame oil
1 spring onion, thinly sliced, to garnish
1 sliced tomato, to garnish
1 sliced cucumber, to garnish
Sprigs of coriander leaves (cilantro), to garnish

Chicken Rice
1 tablespoon oil or chicken fat
1 clove garlic, unpeeled
1 slice of fresh ginger, peeled and bruised
2 cups (400 g) uncooked long-grain rice, rinsed and drained
2 pandanus leaves, tied in a knot (optional)

Sauces
1 portion Chilli Ginger Sauce (page 31)
5 cm (2 in) fresh ginger ground with 1 tablespoon water
2 tablespoons black soy sauce

1 Make the Chilli Ginger Sauce by following the instructions on page 31.
2 Bring the chicken stock to a rolling boil in a pot and add the chicken. Turn off the heat, cover the pan and let the chicken steep for 15 minutes. Then remove the chicken from the stock, plunge it in ice water to cool for 1 minute, and drain. Bring the stock back to a boil, return the chicken to the pot and repeat the steeping process another 3 times so that the chicken has a total of 60 minutes of steeping in the stock. Remove the chicken and set aside to cool. Keep the stock warm to cook the Chicken Rice. When cool enough to handle, cut the chicken into serving pieces. Drizzle the soy sauce and sesame oil over and garnish with coriander leaves.
3 To cook the Chicken Rice, heat the oil in a pan over medium to high heat and brown the garlic and ginger, about 1 minute. Add the rice and stir-fry until fragrant, about 2 minutes. Add the pandanus leaves, if using, and 4 cups (1 litre) of the reserved stock, and bring it to a boil. Reduce the heat and simmer, covered, for 15 to 20 minutes until the rice is cooked. Alternatively, cook the seasoned rice in a rice cooker.
4 Place each of the Sauces in separate serving dishes. Pour the remaining chicken stock into small individual bowls and garnish with freshly sliced spring onion. Serve the chicken with the hot Chicken Rice, Sauces, sliced tomato and cucumber, and small bowls of the chicken stock on the side.

Serves 4–6   Preparation time: 25 mins   Cooking time: 1 hour 25 mins

Laksa Noodle Soup   Mixed Seafood and Noodles in Spicy Coconut Broth

Laksa incorporates both Chinese and Malay cooking styles with a remarkable result—fresh rice noodles bathed in spicy coconut milk curry with chunks of seafood, egg and deep-fried tofu, and a sprinkling of fragrant herbs.

3 tablespoons oil
3 cups (750 ml) thin coconut milk
  or 1 cup (250 ml) coconut cream
  mixed with 2 cups (500 ml) water
2 cups (500 ml) chicken stock or
  1 teaspoon chicken stock granules
  dissolved in 2 cups (500 ml)
  hot water
250 g (8 oz) medium fresh prawns,
  shelled and deveined
100 g (3½ oz) squid, cleaned,
  skinned and sliced (optional)
6 fresh scallops (optional)
4 cakes deep-fried tofu or *aburage*
  (about 50 g/2 oz), cut into 8 pieces
¼ teaspoon salt
¼ teaspoon ground white pepper
400 g (14 oz) fresh laksa noodles
  (rice noodles), blanched in boiling
  water, or 200 g (7 oz) dried rice vermicelli (*beehoon*), soaked in water
  to soften
1 cup (75 g) bean sprouts, rinsed
  and blanched in boiling water
4 quail eggs, hard-boiled and halved,
  or 2 chicken eggs, hard-boiled and
  quartered
2 sprigs laksa leaves (*daun kesum* or
  polygonum), coarsely chopped, to
  garnish
Crispy Fried Shallots (page 31), to
  garnish (optional)
Small limes (*limau kasturi*) or regular
  limes, cut into wedges, to serve

Spice Paste
1 teaspoon fish curry powder
½ tablespoon ground coriander
2 tablespoons dried prawns, soaked
  in water to soften
8 candlenuts, roughly chopped
2½ cm (1 in) fresh turmeric root,
  peeled and sliced, or 1 teaspoon
  ground turmeric
4 red finger-length chillies, deseeded
  and sliced
5 cm (2 in) fresh ginger, peeled and
  sliced
20 shallots, peeled
5 cloves garlic, peeled
1 tablespoon *belachan* (dried prawn
  paste)
1 teaspoon salt
1 tablespoon sugar (optional)
2 stalks lemongrass, thick bottom
  third only, outer layers removed,
  inner part bruised

> Note: The **coconut milk curry** can be prepared several hours in advance and reheated just before serving. Although laksa leaves (polygonum or Vietnamese mint) add a distinctive touch, omit if not available as nothing else tastes like this pungent herb. Substitute with plain curry powder if fish curry powder is unavailable.

1 To prepare the Spice Paste, grind all the ingredients, except the salt, sugar and lemongrass in a mortar or blender, adding a little oil if necessary to keep the blades turning. Season the paste with the salt and sugar, and set aside with the lemongrass.
2 Heat the oil in a wok or pot over low heat and stir-fry the Spice Paste for 5 minutes until fragrant. Add the coconut milk and chicken stock, and bring to a boil, stirring constantly. Then reduce the heat, add all the seafood and the tofu, and season with the salt and pepper. Simmer until cooked, about 3 minutes. Then remove the coconut curry from the heat.
3 To serve, distribute the noodles and bean sprouts into 4 serving bowls and ladle the hot curry with the seafood and tofu over the noodles to fill each bowl. Garnish with the eggs, laksa leaves and Crispy Fried Shallots, and serve the lime wedges on the side.

Serves 4   Preparation time: 40 mins   Cooking time: 30 mins

Fried Beehoon   Rice Vermicelli Stir-fried with Mushrooms and Vegetables

A simple light dish that can be eaten as a snack or as part of a main meal.

10 dried black Chinese mushrooms
1 tablespoon oyster sauce
$1/2$ tablespoon sugar
10–15 fresh or canned button mushrooms, rinsed and halved
4 tablespoons oil
8 cloves garlic, minced
1 onion, sliced
1 carrot, sliced into thin shreds
250 g (8 oz) dried rice vermicelli (beehoon), soaked in hot water to soften
2 tablespoons soy sauce
1 teaspoon black soy sauce
$1/2$ teaspoon salt
$1/2$ teaspoon pepper
1 heaping cup chopped chye sim, bok choy or cabbage
2 cups (150 g) bean sprouts
2 red finger-length chillies, thinly sliced, to serve
Small limes (limau kasturi) or regular limes, halved, to serve (optional)

1 Soak the dried black Chinese mushrooms in $4/5$ cup (200 ml) hot water for 10 minutes to soften. Then discard the stems and thinly slice the caps. Reserve the soaking water.
2 Combine the oyster sauce and sugar in a bowl. Add all the mushrooms, mix well and set aside to marinate for 5 to 10 minutes.
3 Heat the oil in a wok and stir-fry the garlic over medium heat until light golden brown, about 1 minute. Add the onion and stir-fry until transparent, about 3 minutes. Then add the marinated mushrooms and stir-fry for 1 minute. Add the carrot and stir-fry briskly for 10 to 20 seconds.
4 Add the softened beehoon and stir-fry briskly for 1 minute. Season with the soy sauces, salt and pepper, and stir-fry briskly for another minute. Then add the chye sim, bean sprouts and reserved mushroom water, and stir-fry for another 2 to 3 minutes until the vegetables are wilted. Serve hot with the chillies and lime halves on the side.

Serves 4   Preparation time: 30 mins   Cooking time: 10 mins

Fried Kway Teow   Char Kway Teow

Fresh flat rice noodles (kway teow) stir-fried with seafood and chilli paste is practically Singapore's national dish.

4 tablespoons oil
5 cloves garlic, minced
100 g ($3^1/2$ oz) red snapper fillet, sliced (optional)
250 g (8 oz) medium fresh prawns, shelled and deveined
200 g (7 oz) squid, cleaned and sliced
1–2 tablespoons chilli paste
2 sweet dried Chinese sausages (lap cheong), blanched and thinly sliced
500 g (1 lb) fresh flat rice noodles (kway teow) or 250 g (8 oz) dried rice sticks, blanched in hot water and drained
1 cup (100 g) chye sim, washed and cut into lengths
1 tablespoon soy sauce
1–2 tablespoons black soy sauce
$1/2$ teaspoon sugar (optional)
3 eggs, lightly beaten
$3/4$ cup (about 60 g) bean sprouts
1 red chilli finger-length, thinly sliced
$1/2$ teaspoon salt
$1/2$ teaspoon ground white pepper

1 Heat 2 tablespoons of the oil in a wok over high heat and stir-fry the garlic until light brown, about 1 minute. Add the seafood, chilli paste and Chinese sausages, and stir-fry for another 2 minutes.
2 Add the noodles and chye sim, and stir. Then season with the soy sauces and sugar, and stir to mix well.
3 Push the noodles to the side of the wok, reduce the heat to medium, add the rest of the oil and the beaten eggs. Scramble the eggs, then stir-fry with the rest of the ingredients in the wok to mix well, about 1 minute.
4 Add the bean sprouts and chilli, and stir-fry for another 1 to 2 minutes. Season with salt and pepper, and serve immediately.

Serves 4–6   Preparation time: 25 mins   Cooking time: 7 mins

Classic Hokkien Mee   Braised Noodles with Seafood Hokkien Style

As the majority of Singapore's Chinese population is Hokkien, this is an all-time favourite noodle dish. A combination of fresh yellow wheat noodles (Hokkien *mee*) and rice vermicelli are stir-fried with a mixture of seafood, vegetables and pork. The whole lot is then bathed in rich stock and seasoned to perfection. Robust rather than refined, it makes an excellent lunch or late-night snack.

250 g (8 oz) medium fresh prawns, shelled and deveined, shells and heads reserved to make stock
1 small squid or fish fillet, cleaned and sliced
$3/_4$ cup (100 g) pork fillet or belly pork, very thinly sliced
2 cups (500 ml) water
$1/_3$ cup (90 ml) oil
4 cloves garlic, minced
250 g (8 oz) fresh yellow wheat noodles (Hokkien *mee*)
150 g (5 oz) dried rice vermicelli (*beehoon*), soaked in hot water to soften, then cut into short lengths
5 stalks *chye sim* or *bok choy* leaves, rinsed and sliced
1 cup (75 g) bean sprouts
2 tablespoons soy sauce
$1/_2$ teaspoon ground white pepper
1 egg, lightly beaten
Fresh coriander leaves (cilantro), chopped, or finely shredded carrot, to garnish (optional)
Sambal Belachan (page 30)
Small limes (*limau kasturi*), halved, to serve

1 Prepare the Sambal Belachan by following the instructions on page 30.
2 Make a stock by placing the prawns, reserved prawn shells and heads, squid or fish, pork and water in a pot and bringing it to a boil for 2 to 3 minutes. Strain and reserve the stock. Set the seafood and meat aside. Discard the prawn shells and heads.
3 Heat the oil in a wok over medium heat, add the garlic and stir-fry for a 1 minute until light brown. Add the prawns, squid and pork, and stir-fry briskly for a few seconds. Then add $1^1/_2$ cups (375 ml) of the stock and simmer for another minute.
4 Increase the heat to high, add both types of noodles, *chye sim*, bean sprouts, soy sauce and pepper. Stir-fry briskly until all ingredients are mixed, about 2 to 3 minutes. Then add the egg and cook for about a minute until the egg is cooked. Garnish with fresh coriander leaves or shredded carrot, if using. Serve with a small bowl of Sambal Belachan and lime halves on the side.

Note: It is essential to cook the noodles over very high heat to ensure that most of the Stock evaporates by the time the noodles are cooked.

Serves 4–6   Preparation time: 30 mins   Cooking time: 10 mins

Mee Siam Rice Noodles in Spicy Tamarind Gravy

This Nonya specialty—noodles in a spicy sweet and sour broth—is a popular snack at food stalls throughout Singapore.

30 dried chillies (about 100 g), cut into lengths, deseeded and soaked in water to soften
3 tablespoons oil
250 g (8 oz) dried rice vermicelli (*beehoon*), soaked in hot water to soften
2 cups (150 g) bean sprouts, rinsed, seed coats and tails removed, or cabbage
4 cakes deep-fried tofu or *aburage* (about 200 g/7 oz total), diced, or 2 cakes pressed tofu (300 g/10 oz), diced and pan-fried until golden brown
250 g (8 oz) medium fresh prawns, boiled for 1 to 2 minutes in 3 cups (750 ml) water, drained, shelled and deveined, prawn stock reserved
8 quail eggs, halved, or 2 hard-boiled eggs, shelled and cut into wedges
2 spring onions or garlic chives (*koo chye*), cut into lengths, to garnish
Sambal Belachan (page 30), to serve
4 small limes (*limau kasturi*), halved, or regular limes to serve

Sauce
5 tablespoons dried prawns, soaked in water to soften
10 candlenuts, roughly chopped
8-10 shallots, peeled
6 cloves garlic, peeled
1 teaspoon *belachan* (dried prawn paste)
5 tablespoons oil
$1/2$ cup (75 g) unsalted peanuts, roasted and coarsely crushed
3 tablespoons black bean paste (*tau cheo*), mashed
6 tablespoons sugar
6 tablespoons tamarind pulp mashed with 1 cup (250 ml) warm water, squeezed and strained for juice
1 stalk lemongrass, thick bottom third only, outer layers removed, inner part bruised
$1/2$ tablespoon black soy sauce
1 teaspoon salt
1 teaspoon pepper

1 Prepare the Sambal Belachan by following the instructions on page 30. Grind the dried chillies to a paste in a blender, transfer to a small bowl and set aside.
2 Prepare the Sauce by grinding the dried prawns, candlenuts, shallots, garlic and *belachan* in a blender, adding a little oil if necessary to keep the blades turning. Heat the oil in a wok over medium heat and and gently stir-fry the ground paste for 5 minutes. Add the peanuts, black bean paste and sugar, and stir-fry for another minute. Add the reserved prawn stock, tamarind juice, lemongrass and soy sauce, and bring to a boil. Reduce the heat and simmer gently, uncovered, for 5 minutes. Season with salt and pepper. Remove from the heat and keep warm.
3 Heat the oil in a wok and stir-fry 3 tablespoons of the reserved chilli paste for 1 minute. Then add the noodles and continue to stir-fry just long enough to coat with the paste so they take on a red colour, about 1 minute.
4 To serve, divide the noodles into 4 serving bowls. Top the noodles with bean sprouts, fried tofu, prawns and eggs. Ladle the hot Sauce over and garnish with spring onions or chives. Serve with a small bowl of Sambal Belachan and lime halves on the side.

Serves 4   Preparation time: 25 mins   Cooking time: 15 mins

Prawn Noodle Soup Hae Mee

The flavour of this relatively simple noodle dish depends on the richly flavoured stock made from both fresh and dried prawns, and pork or chicken. This soup is traditionally served with delicious, crunchy pork cracklings; some may omit these for health reasons but they make all the difference to the flavour of the dish.

8 cups (2 litres) water
250 g (8 oz) large fresh prawns,
  shelled and deveined, heads and
  shells reserved for the Stock
50 g (2 oz) back pork fat
  or salt pork, cubed (optional)
500 g (1 lb) fresh yellow wheat
  noodles (Hokkien *mee*)
1 cup (75 g) bean sprouts, rinsed,
  or a few leafy greens
1 spring onion, thinly sliced,
  to garnish
Ground white pepper, to taste

Stock
1 tablespoon oil
100 g (3^1/$_2$ oz) small fresh prawns
3 tablespoons dried prawns
1 dried chilli, whole (optional)
5 shallots, diced
5 cloves garlic, minced
10 whole white peppercorns, coarsely
  ground and dry-fried until fragrant
250 g (8 oz) pork or chicken bones
1 tablespoon sugar
^{1}/$_4$ teaspoon salt

1 Bring the water to a boil in a pot, add the shelled prawns and boil for 2 minutes until the prawns turn pink. Drain the prawns and set aside, reserving the prawn broth to make the Stock.

2 To make the Stock, heat the oil in a pot over medium to low heat and stir-fry the reserved prawn heads and shells with the small fresh prawns, dried prawns and dried chilli for 5 minutes. Crush the ingredients in the pot firmly with the back of a wooden spoon against the side of the pan, then add all the other Stock ingredients, except the sugar and salt, and add the reserved prawn broth. Simmer gently over low heat, uncovered, for 20 minutes until the liquid is reduced to three-quarters of the original amount.

3 Heat the sugar in a small skillet with 1 tablespoon of water and cook, stirring constantly, over medium heat until it caramelises, about 1 minute. Add this caramel syrup to the Stock and mix well. Remove from the heat and strain the Stock, pressing the solids firmly with the back of a spoon to extract all the liquid, then season with the salt. Keep the Stock hot if using immediately.

4 While the Stock is cooking, fry the pork fat, if using, in a wok over medium to low heat until the oil runs out and the pork is crisp and golden, about 3 to 5 minutes. Drain and set aside. Alternatively, place the pork fat in a preheated oven at 180°C (350°F) and bake it for 5 to 10 minutes until crisp and the oil runs out.

5 Scald the noodles in boiling water for 1 minute to heat through, then divide them into 4 serving bowls. Top each serving with bean sprouts or leafy greens, ladle the hot Stock over and add some prawns into each bowl. Sprinkle the fried pork, spring onion and add a liberal dash of white pepper. Serve immediately with sliced red chilli in a bowl of soy sauce or with the sambal of your choice.

Serves 4   Preparation time: 25 mins   Cooking time: 30 mins

Soto Ayam   Spicy Chicken with Noodles

As the ancestors of many Malay Singaporeans originally came from Java, it's not surprising that this Javanese noodle soup is found at most Singapore food centres. It's ideal as a light luncheon dish or even as a starter.

1 large fresh chicken (about $1^1/_2$ kg/3 lbs)
8 cups (2 litres) water
1 teaspoon salt
1 teaspoon pepper
50 g (2 oz) dried glass noodles, soaked in hot water to soften, then drained
6 slices of Lontong (page 31), cubed,
  or 2 cups (400 g) cold cooked rice (optional)
6 quail eggs, peeled and halved, or 5 hard-boiled eggs, peeled and quartered
$1^1/_2$ cups (125 g) bean sprouts, rinsed
5 tablespoons coarsely chopped Chinese celery or parsley leaves
Crispy Fried Shallots (page 31), to garnish
Sambal Belachan (page 30), to serve
3 small limes (*limau kasturi*) or regular, halved, to serve

Spice Paste
8 candlenuts, roughly chopped
6 cm ($2^1/_2$ in) fresh turmeric root, peeled and sliced,
  or 2 teaspoons ground turmeric
5 cm (2 in) fresh ginger, peeled and sliced
24 shallots, peeled
10 cloves garlic, peeled
3 tablespoons oil
3 stalks lemongrass, thick bottom third only, outer layers removed,
  inner part bruised
5 cm (2 in) fresh galangal root, peeled and sliced
8 kaffir lime leaves
2 tablespoons ground coriander

1 Prepare the Lontong, Crispy Fried Shallots and Sambal Belachan by following the instructions on pages 30 and 31.
2 Place the chicken and water in a pot and simmer over low heat for 30 minutes.
3 While the chicken is simmering, make the Spice Paste. Grind the candlenuts, turmeric, ginger, shallots and garlic in a blender until fine, adding a little oil if necessary to keep the blades turning. Heat the oil in a wok and stir-fry the ground paste with the remaining Spice Paste ingredients for 4 to 5 minutes until fragrant.
4 Add the cooked Spice Paste to the pot with the chicken and continue to simmer for another 20 minutes until the chicken is cooked. Season with salt and pepper, and remove from the heat. Remove the chicken from the stock, and set aside to cool. When cool enough to handle, debone the chicken and shred the meat into long strips. Strain the stock well, and return it to the pot to keep warm.
5 Portion the noodles, Lontong or cooked rice, chicken strips, hard-boiled eggs, bean sprouts and celery leaves into 6 serving bowls. Fill each bowl with the warm stock and garnish with the Crispy Fried Shallots. Serve hot with a bowl of Sambal Belachan and lime halves on the side.

Serves 6   Preparation time: 30 mins   Cooking time: 1 hour

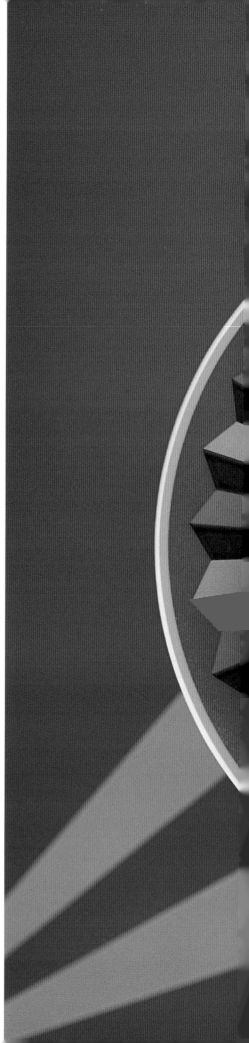

Indian Mee Goreng   Indian Fried Noodles

Although noodles were brought to Singapore by the Chinese, all the other ethnic groups have enthusiastically adopted and adapted them to suit their tastes. This spicy dish—which you cannot find in India—is well-balanced by the sweetness of fresh tomatoes and tomato sauce.

4 tablespoons oil
1 cake firm or pressed tofu (250 g/8 oz total), drained and cubed
6–8 dried chillies, cut into lengths and soaked in warm water to soften, then ground to a paste, or 3–5 tablespoons chilli powder
5 cloves garlic, minced
1 teaspoon *belachan* (dried prawn paste)
150 g (5 oz) boneless chicken or lamb, thinly sliced
150 g (5 oz) medium fresh prawns, peeled and deveined
400 g (12 oz) fresh yellow wheat noodles (Hokkien *mee*)
2 cups (200 g) *chye sim*, washed and sliced
2 tablespoons soy sauce
3 tablespoons tomato ketchup
$1/2$ teaspoon salt
$1/2$ cup (125 ml) chicken stock or $1/4$ teaspoon chicken stock granules dissolved in $1/2$ cup (125 ml) hot water
2 eggs, beaten
1 onion, diced
1 tomato, diced, or 2 tablespoons tomato purée
1 red finger-length chilli, sliced
1 green finger-length chilli, sliced
2 cups (150 g) bean sprouts, seed coats and tails discarded
$1/2$ teaspoon ground white pepper

Garnishes
Coriander leaves (cilantro) or Chinese celery, coarsely chopped
Spring onions, sliced (optional)
Crispy Fried Shallots (page 31), (optional)
Small limes (*limau kasturi*), halved

1 Heat 2 tablespoons of the oil in a large wok and stir-fry the tofu cubes over medium heat until golden brown, about 7 minutes. Remove from the oil and set aside to drain on paper towels.

2 In the same wok, add the rest of the oil and stir-fry 3 to 5 tablespoons of the chilli paste or the chilli powder with the garlic and *belachan* for 3 minutes until fragrant. Add the sliced chicken or lamb and stir-fry until it turns opaque, about 3 minutes. Then add the prawns and stir-fry until the prawns are cooked, another 2 minutes.

3 Add the noodles and *chye sim*, mix well, and cook for 1 minute. Then add the soy sauce, tomato ketchup, salt and chicken stock, and cook for 3 minutes until the liquid is absorbed by the noodles and the mixture is dry.

4 Push the noodles to one side of the wok with the spatula. Add the eggs and scramble. Then stir the noodles and the eggs together until the eggs are cooked. (Add a little more chicken stock for a moister Mee Goreng.)

5 Add the onion, tomato, fresh chillies and bean sprouts, and stir-fry for 3 minutes. Then add the fried tofu and mix well until heated through. Season with the ground pepper. Garnish with coriander leaves, spring onions, Crispy Fried Shallots and serve fresh limes on the side.

Note: If preferred, substitute spinach or cabbage for the *chye sim*.

Serves 6   Preparation time: 35 mins   Cooking time: 15 mins

Lontong Sayur Lemak

Vegetables in Coconut Milk with Compressed Rice

This seasoned vegetable stew with Lontong is served as part of a main meal or as a meal on its own for breakfast or lunch.

2 cakes pressed tofu, about 500 g (1 lb), cubed and deep-fried
2 cups (500 ml) thick coconut milk or 1 cup (250 ml) coconut cream
  mixed with 1 cup (250 ml) water
1 teaspoon salt
1 teaspoon freshly ground black pepper
1 portion Lontong (page 31)

Spice Paste
3 tablespoons dried prawns, soaked in water to soften
1 tablespoon ground coriander
$2^1/_2$ cm (1 in) fresh galangal root, peeled and sliced
5 cm (2 in) fresh turmeric root, peeled and sliced,
  or 2 teaspoons ground turmeric
10–15 red finger-length chillies, deseeded and sliced
20 shallots, peeled
10 cloves garlic, peeled
4 tablespoons oil
1 teaspoon *belachan* (dried prawn paste), roasted (page 22)

Vegetables
1 slender Asian eggplant (about 200 g/7 oz), sliced crosswise
1 carrot, peeled and sliced crosswise
200 g (7 oz) sweet potatoes, jicama or chayote, cut into chunks
20 green beans, cut into lengths

1 Prepare the Lontong by following the instructions on page 31. Unwrap the Lontong from the banana leaf or cheesecloth and slice into chunks. Set aside.
2 To make the Spice Paste, grind the dried prawns, coriander, galangal, turmeric, chillies, shallots and garlic in a mortar or blender until fine, adding a little oil if necessary to keep the blades turning. Heat the oil in a wok and stir-fry the *belachan* and the ground paste 5 to 7 minutes until fragrant. Transfer the Spice Paste to a small bowl and set aside.
3 To prepare the Vegetables, bring 3 cups (750 ml) water to a boil in a pot and parboil the vegetables, about 5 minutes. Add the Spice Paste and simmer for another 5 minutes. Add the tofu, simmer a minute longer, then add the coconut milk or cream. Cook, stirring, until the oil separates from the milk, about 3 to 5 minutes. Season with the salt and pepper, and serve hot with Lontong.

Serves 6–8   Preparation time: 25 mins   Cooking time: 25 mins

Special Nonya Fried Rice

This version of fried rice from a Nonya kitchen gets its distinctive flavour from the tiny dried salted fish used by Chinese cooks. Smaller than the usual Malay *ikan bilis*, they are sometimes called silverfish.

3 tablespoons oil
$1/_2$ cup (80 g) very small dried salted fish or bits of salted fish
3 cloves garlic, minced
1 chicken breast (about 125 g/4 oz), diced
150 g (5 oz) medium fresh prawns, peeled and deveined
3 eggs, beaten
4 cups (800 g) cold cooked rice or leftover rice
1 tablespoon soy sauce
$1/_2$ teaspoon salt
$1/_2$ teaspoon pepper
$1/_4$ teaspoon sesame oil (optional)
1 cup (75 g) bean sprouts
2 spring onions, thinly sliced

1 Heat the oil in a wok and stir-fry the dried salted fish until brown and crispy. Remove from the oil and set aside to drain.
2 In the same wok, gently stir-fry the garlic for a few seconds, then add the chicken and prawns, and stir-fry for 3 to 4 minutes. Increase the heat and add the eggs, stirring until the eggs are cooked.
3 Add the rice and stir-fry over high heat until the rice is heated through. Then add the rest of the ingredients and stir-fry for another 3 minutes. Add the crispy silverfish or salted fish and stir to mix well. Serve immediately.

Note: Leftover rice kept overnight is preferred for any fried rice dish, as it is drier and firmer, and will result in a better textured fried rice dish.

Serves 4   Preparation time: 15 mins   Cooking time: 10 mins

Honey Barbecued Chicken Wings

1 kg (2 lbs) chicken wings (about 10 large chicken wings)
2 tablespoons oyster sauce
2 tablespoons honey
2 tablespoons rice wine or sherry
2 tablespoons soy sauce
1 tablespoon black soy sauce
1 teaspoon sesame oil
1 teaspoon freshly ground black pepper
$1/_4$ teaspoon salt (optional)

Mix all the ingredients in a large bowl, cover and marinate in the refrigerator for 6 hours or overnight. Cook over hot charcoal, under a broiler or in a pre-heated oven at 220°C (440°F) for 10 to 20 minutes until the chicken is cooked and golden brown.

Serves 4   Preparation time: 10 mins + marination time   Cooking time: 20 mins

Popiah   Hokkien-style Fresh Spring Rolls

Hokkien-style Popiah are normally made using very thin fresh wrappers made from rice and wheat flour and water. Assemble Popiah just before serving, as otherwise they go soggy, or place all the prepared ingredients on the table and allow your guests to create their own in an informal gathering. A Popiah party is always a big hit!

1 tablespoon oil
4 cloves garlic, peeled and crushed
2 shallots, sliced
1 medium *bangkuang* (jicama) (about 600 g/20 oz), peeled and sliced into matchsticks
$1/_4$ teaspoon five spice powder
$1/_2$ teaspoon sugar
$3/_4$ teaspoon salt
$1/_2$ teaspoon freshly ground white pepper
6 soft lettuce leaves, washed and dried
1 tablespoon sweet black sauce
10 cloves garlic, minced
4 red finger-length chillies, deseeded and ground to a paste with $1/_4$ teaspoon salt, or 1 red finger-length chilli, sliced
1 shallot, minced
$2/_3$ cup (50 g) bean sprouts, rinsed and blanched in boiling water
$1/_2$ cup (60 g) cooked crabmeat
250 g (8 oz) medium fresh prawns, peeled, deveined, halved lengthwise and poached for 1 minute
1 hard-boiled egg, halved lengthwise then sliced crosswise
1 sweet dried Chinese sausage (*lap cheong*), thinly sliced and blanched in hot water

Popiah Wrappers
$1/_2$ cup (75 g) rice flour
$1^1/_2$ tablespoons plain flour
$1/_4$ teaspoon salt
2 eggs
$1/_2$ teaspoon oil
1 cup (250 ml) water

1 First prepare the Popiah Wrappers by sifting the flours and salt together into a bowl. In another bowl, mix the eggs, oil and water. Add the flour mixture a little at time, mixing well to obtain a smooth batter. Set the batter aside in the refrigerator for at least 1 hour.
2 Grease a nonstick pan with oil. Ladle 2 tablespoons of the batter onto the pan and swirl it quickly to make a very thin pancake. Cook over medium heat until the batter sets, about 2 minutes. Place the cooked wrapper on a plate. Repeat until all the batter is used up.
3 To prepare the filling, heat the oil in a wok and stir-fry the garlic, shallots and *bangkuang* over medium heat for 5 minutes until the *bangkuang* is soft. Season with the five spice powder, sugar, salt and pepper. Set aside to cool.
4 To assemble, place a fresh Popiah Wrapper on a plate. Place a lettuce leaf on the wrapper and smear a little of the sweet black sauce and minced garlic on it. Then add a little of the chilli paste or sliced chilli and shallot. Strain 2 heaping tablespoons of the *bangkuang* filling between two spoons to press out the liquid, and place it on the lettuce. Add a sprinkling of bean sprouts, crabmeat, prawns, egg and Chinese sausage. Tuck in the sides of the wrapper and roll it up firmly. Repeat with the rest of the wrappers and filling to make another 5 Popiah. Halve or slice each Popiah into 3 pieces and serve.

Note: If it's too time-consuming to prepare fresh Popiah Wrappers, you may be able to find packets of Popiah Wrappers in the refrigerator or freezer section in some supermarkets. Or substitute Filipino lumpia wrappers lightly cooked in a nonstick pan with a little oil, or burrito wrappers. If you cannot find *bangkuang* (jicama), you may substitute a mixture of daikon radish and cabbage, both very thinly sliced.

Makes 6 Popiah   Preparation time: 35 mins + 10 mins assembling time
Cooking time: 45 mins

Pork Satay with Pineapple Sauce   Sate Babi

Skewers of seasoned meat or chicken grilled over charcoal is one of Singapore's most popular dishes. This local Chinese version is made with pork and served with a rich peanut sauce flavoured with crushed pineapple.

500 g (1 lb) pork fillet, cut into bite-
   sized cubes
18 bamboo skewers
1 portion Pineapple Satay Sauce
   (page 30)

Marinade
1$^{1}/_{2}$ tablespoons coriander seeds,
   or 2 teaspoons ground coriander
2 teaspoons brown sugar
1 cm ($^{1}/_{2}$ in) fresh turmeric root,
   peeled and sliced, or $^{1}/_{2}$ teaspoon
   ground turmeric
1 teaspoon salt
1 stalk lemongrass, thick bottom part
   only, outer layers removed, inner
   part sliced
4 tablespoons oil

1 Prepare the Pineapple Satay Sauce by following the instructions on page 30.
2 To make the Marinade, grind all the ingredients in a mortar or blender, adding the oil to keep the blades turning. Rub the Marinade into the pork cubes and set aside to marinate for 2 hours. In the meantime, soak the skewers in cold water to prevent them from burning during grilling.
3 Thread 3 pork cubes onto each bamboo skewer until all the meat and skewers are used up. Then brush with a little oil and cook over hot charcoal or under a broiler, turning from time to time and brushing with more oil, until the meat is browned evenly on the outside and well cooked on the inside, about 5 to 7 minutes. Serve with a bowl of the Pineapple Satay Sauce and, if desired, chunks of fresh pineapple, cucumber and raw onions or shallots on the side.

Makes 18 skewers   Preparation time: 40 mins + marination time
Cooking time: 20 mins

Malay Chicken Satay   Sate Ayam

The tantalising aroma of seasoned meat roasting over a charcoal fire, anointed from time to time with a "brush" of fragrant lemongrass oil, is irresistible. It's no wonder this dish is an all-time favourite.

4 chicken legs, deboned and cut into
  2-cm (³/₄-in) cubes
12 skewers soaked in water for 1 hour
1 stalk lemongrass, thick end bruised,
  for brushing
Oil for basting
1 portion Satay Sauce (page 30)

Spice Paste
1 tablespoon coriander seeds
2 stalks lemongrass, thick bottom
  third only, outer layers removed,
  inner part sliced
5 shallots, peeled
2 cloves garlic, peeled
¹/₂ teaspoon chilli powder
2 tablespoons sugar
¹/₂ teaspoon salt
1 teaspoon ground turmeric
2 tablespoons oil

1 Prepare the Satay Sauce by following the instructions on page 30.
2 To make the Spice Paste, grind the ingredients in a mortar or blender, adding the oil to keep the blades turning. Mix the paste with the chicken cubes and marinate for at least 12 hours.
3 Thread 4 to 5 pieces of the chicken onto each skewer until all the chicken pieces are used up. Grill the chicken over a hot charcoal fire or under a broiler, constantly brushing with the stalk of lemongrass dipped in the oil. Turn the skewers frequently to prevent the meat from burning. The chicken should be evenly browned on the outside and just cooked on the inside.
4 Serve with a bowl of Satay Sauce and sliced cucumber, raw onion and Lontong or boiled rice on the side.

Note: Ketupat are compressed rice cakes similar to Lontong (page 31). They are cooked in beautifully woven cases of coconut leaves or *daun palas* (see photo above). The rice takes the shape of the case and is usually served quartered. These traditional festive cakes dress every table during Malay celebrations in Singapore.

Makes 12 sticks   Preparation time: 30 mins + marination time
Cooking time: 10 mins

Fruit and Vegetable Rojak   Salad with Spicy Peanut Sauce

An unusual salad of tropical fruits and raw vegetables drenched in a pungent peanut sauce. *Hay koh* (fermented prawn sauce), sometimes referred to by its Indonesian name, *petis*, makes all the difference to this dish.

1 unripe mango (about 200 g/7oz), peeled, pitted and sliced

1/4 fresh pineapple (about 250 g/8 oz), sliced into small chunks

1 small lime (*limau kasturi*), thinly sliced

1 *bangkuang* (jicama) (500 g/1 lb), peeled and sliced

250 g (8 oz) *kangkung* (water spinach), washed well, tough bottom of stems discarded, tender stems and leaves blanched in boiling water and drained

1 small cucumber, sliced

2 cups (150 g) bean sprouts, rinsed and blanched in boiling water

4 cakes deep-fried tofu or *aburage* (about 50 g/2 oz), cubed

2 Chinese crullers, cut into 6–8 pieces (optional, see note)

1 wild ginger bud, very thinly sliced (optional)

Roasted peanuts, coarsely crushed, to garnish (optional)

Peanut Rojak Sauce

1 cup (100 g) roasted unsalted peanuts, skins removed, or 10 heaped tablespoons crunchy peanut butter

1/2 teaspoon *belachan* (dried prawn paste), roasted (page 22)

3–5 red finger-length chillies, deseeded and sliced

2 *chili padi* (bird's-eye chillies), deseeded and sliced (optional)

3 tablespoons *hay koh* (fermented prawn sauce)

2 heaped tablespoons tamarind pulp mashed with 1/2 cup (125 ml) warm water, squeezed and strained to obtain juice

2–3 tablespoons shaved palm sugar

1/2 teaspoon salt

1 To make the Peanut Rojak Sauce, grind all the ingredients in a mortar or blender until fine and set aside.

2 Place the prepared mango, pineapple and lime in a mixing bowl, add a little Peanut Rojak Sauce and mix well. Then add the *bangkuang*, *kangkung*, cucumber, bean sprouts and a little more Sauce, and mix well again. Repeat with the tofu, crullers and ginger bud. Top with a generous helping of crushed peanuts, if using, and serve. Alternatively, spoon the Peanut Rojak Sauce onto individual serving plates and arrange the prepared fruits, vegetables, tofu and crullers over it. Serve garnished with ginger bud and roasted peanuts, if using (see photo).

Note: Chinese crullers (*yu tiaow*) are 2 long sticks of dough stuck together and then deep-fried. Sometimes called Chinese doughnuts (*yu char kway*), they are savoury rather than sweet and are traditionally eaten with rice porridge (*congee*). They are available in Asian fresh markets. Omit if unavailable. *Hay koh* (fermented prawn sauce) has a strong fishy taste and takes some getting used to. It is sold in jars in supermarkets and provision shops.

Serves 6   Preparation time: 30 mins

Tauhu Goreng

Deep-fried Tofu Salad with Spicy Peanut Dressing

A popular dish at food stalls in Singapore, especially in the morning, the fried tofu is usually halved diagonally and stuffed with a mixture of blanched bean sprouts and raw cucumber, and drizzled with a delicious Spicy Peanut Dressing.

2 cakes pressed tofu or firm tofu (about 500 g/1 lb total)
Oil for shallow-frying (about 3 tablespoons)
1 cup (75 g) bean sprouts, rinsed and blanched in boiling water, then drained
1 small cucumber, sliced into thin shreds
2 spring onions, sliced into thin shreds, to garnish (optional)
Coriander leaves (cilantro), to garnish (optional)

Spicy Peanut Dressing
2 tablespoons oil
8 shallots, sliced
5 cloves garlic, sliced
2–5 red finger-length chillies, deseeded and sliced
$\frac{1}{2}$ teaspoon *belachan* (dried prawn paste)
2 tablespoons sweet black sauce
2 heaped tablespoons tamarind pulp mashed with 1 cup (250 ml) warm water, squeezed and strained for juice
1 cup (175 g) coarsely crushed fried or roasted peanuts, or 10 heaped tablespoons crunchy peanut butter

1 To prepare the Spicy Peanut Dressing, heat the oil in a saucepan and stir-fry the shallots, garlic, chillies and *belachan* for 5 minutes until fragrant. Then add the sweet black sauce and tamarind juice, and cook for another minute. Remove from the heat and set aside to cool. When cooled, grind the mixture to a paste in a mortar or blender. Add the crushed peanuts or peanut butter and mix well.

2 Shallow-fry the tofu in about 1 cm ($\frac{1}{2}$ in) of oil over medium heat in a skillet until light golden brown, about 3 minutes on each side. Remove from the oil and set aside to drain and cool. When cool enough to handle, cut the tofu into bite-sized pieces.

3 To assemble, arrange the bean sprouts, cucumber and spring onions (if using) on a plate. Top with the fried tofu and pour the dressing over. Serve garnished with coriander leaves. Alternatively, serve the dressing in a small bowl on the side with another bowl of freshly sliced spring onions if desired.

Note: To save time, prepare the Spicy Peanut Dressing in advance. If sweet black sauce is not available, substitute black soy sauce sweetened with sugar.

Serves 4   Preparation time: 20 mins   Cooking time: 10 mins

Murtabak   Indian Flatbread Stuffed with Spicy Minced Meat and Onion

An Indian Muslim dish universally loved in Singapore, Murtabak is a feather-light pancake filled with minced meat and fried on a hot griddle. Mutton would be the usual choice in Singapore, although lamb, beef or chicken may be used instead. The texture of the dough is light and crispy, the filling wonderfully satisfying—great as an appetiser or a late-night snack.

3 tablespoons ghee or oil for frying
Thinly sliced red or green finger-
  length chillies (optional)

Dough
3 cups (450 g) plain flour
Scant $1/2$ cup (125 ml) fresh milk
Scant $1/2$ cup (125 ml) water
1 egg, lightly beaten
$1/2$ teaspoon sugar
$1/2$ teaspoon salt
2 teaspoons softened butter

Filling
2 tablespoons oil
10 cloves garlic, minced
2 onions, diced
2 cups (500 g/1 lb) minced lamb,
  chicken or beef
$1^1/2$ tablespoons meat curry powder
1 teaspoon ground turmeric
$1/2$ teaspoon chilli powder
$1/2$ teaspoon salt
$1/4$ teaspoon ground white pepper
1 stalk Chinese leek or celery, very
  thinly sliced
6 eggs, lightly beaten

1 To make the Dough, mix all the ingredients, except the butter, in a bowl and knead for 10 minutes to form a smooth Dough. Roll the Dough into a ball, place in a dry bowl, cover and set aside to rest in a warm place for at least 1 hour.

2 To prepare the Filling, heat the oil in a wok or skillet and stir-fry the garlic and onions until they are transparent and fragrant, about 5 minutes. Add the minced meat, curry powder, turmeric and chilli powder, and stir-fry for another 2 to 3 minutes. Season with the salt and pepper. Remove from the heat and set aside to cool. Once the meat mixture has cooled, add the leek or celery and beaten eggs, and mix well. Set aside.

3 Half an hour before serving, portion the Dough into 6 equal parts and knead each portion with a little softened butter until smooth. Shape each portion into a ball and set aside again. Roll out each portion of Dough as thinly as possible and cover with a cloth.

4 Heat a heavy iron griddle or large skillet until very hot and grease with a little ghee or oil. Place the rolled out Dough on the griddle, reduce the heat to medium and cook for 1 minute. Then spread one-sixth of the Filling over the Dough. Fold over two opposite sides of the Dough, overlapping slightly, and repeat with the other two sides to make a small rectangular package enclosing the Filling. Cook for 2 to 3 minutes until the Dough is golden brown, then flip it over and cook on the other side. Remove from the heat and set aside to cool on a serving platter. Repeat with the remaining Dough and Filling.

5 Garnish the Murtabak with sliced chillies if using. Serve hot with a bowl of your favourite curry sauce on the side and chase with hot coffee or tea.

Note: The trick to making a good crispy Murtabak is for the Dough to be as thin as possible when cooked, so that it lightly encloses the Filling like a wafer-thin wrapper. Indian chefs twirl the Dough in the air to achieve this. To accompany the Murtabak and curry, serve a refreshing side dish of **Cucumber and Onion Achar**. Slice $1/2$ cucumber and 1 onion, sprinkle $1/4$ teaspoon salt and set aside in a colander for 1 hour to drain. Then rinse and pat dry to remove as much moisture as possible. Refresh the cucumber and onion with a dash of fresh lime or lemon juice and serve.

Makes 6 Murtabak   Preparation time: 30 mins   Cooking time: 1 hour

Singapore Chilli Crab

Another Singapore original—a spicy and sweet tomato sauce, enhancing the delicious taste of fresh crabs. Sold in hawker centres and seafood restaurants in the country, and not to be missed when visiting the island state.

3 fresh crabs (about 2$\frac{1}{2}$ kg/5 lbs total)
Oil for deep-frying
1 cup (250 ml) chicken stock or $\frac{1}{4}$
   teaspoon chicken stock granules
   dissolved in 1 cup (250 ml) hot water
1 egg, lightly beaten
1 tablespoon cornstarch dissolved in
   3 tablespoons water
$\frac{1}{2}$ teaspoon salt
1 teaspoon white pepper
1 spring onion, thinly sliced, to garnish

Sauce
4 tablespoons oil
8 cloves garlic, minced
1 large onion, diced
5 cm (2 in) young ginger, sliced
2 teaspoons black bean paste (*tau cheo*)
3–5 red finger-length chillies,
   deseeded and sliced
2 tomatoes, diced
4 tablespoons sweet bottled chilli sauce
4 tablespoons bottled tomato ketchup
1 teaspoon sesame oil
1 tablespoon soy sauce
1 tablespoon sugar
1 teaspoon chilli powder (optional)
$\frac{1}{2}$ teaspoon ground white pepper

1 Clean and quarter the crabs, cracking the pincers to allow the flavours to penetrate. Pat dry, then deep-fry the crabs in 2 batches in hot oil in a wok for 3 minutes until the shells turn bright red. Remove from the heat and set aside to drain.

2 To make the Sauce, drain the oil in the wok and pour 4 tablespoons of fresh oil into it. Stir-fry the garlic, onion, ginger, black bean paste and chillies over high heat until fragrant, about 1 to 2 minutes. Add the tomatoes, chilli sauce, tomato ketchup, sesame oil, soy sauce and sugar, and mix well. Then reduce the heat and simmer for 1 minute. Add the chilli powder, if using, and season with the pepper.

3 Return the crabs to the wok and toss to coat with the Sauce. Add the chicken stock and cook over high heat for 3 minutes. Add the egg and cornstarch, and stir until the Sauce thickens, about 1 minute. Season with the salt and pepper. Garnish with the freshly sliced spring onion and serve immediately.

Serves 4–6   Preparation time: 30 mins   Cooking time: 15 mins

Black Pepper Crab or Crayfish

1 cup (250 ml) olive oil for stir-frying
2 kg (4 lbs) fresh crabs, crayfish,
   spiny or rock lobster, or large
   prawns, halved lengthwise
1 spring onion, thinly sliced, to garnish

Sauce
5 tablespoons butter
7 cloves garlic, minced
2$\frac{1}{2}$ cm (1 in) fresh ginger, peeled
   and slivered
7 red finger-length chillies, deseeded
   and thinly sliced
2 tablespoons oyster sauce
2 tablespoons soy sauce
2 teaspoons black soy sauce
4 teaspoons sugar
3 tablespoons crushed black pepper

1 Heat half of the olive oil in a wok over high heat and stir-fry half of the crabs or crayfish for 3 minutes. Cover, and cook for 8 minutes until the shells change colour. Remove the cooked shellfish from the oil and set aside to drain. Then repeat with the second batch.

2 To make the Sauce, heat the butter and 2 teaspoons oil in a wok over low heat, add the garlic and ginger, and sauté gently until golden brown, about 3 to 5 minutes. Add the chillies and sauté for another 2 minutes. Add the oyster sauce, both soy sauces and sugar, and simmer over low heat for 30 seconds, then season with the pepper.

3 Cook until the Sauce thickens, about 1 to 2 minutes, then return the shellfish to the wok. Toss to coat well with the Sauce and cook for another 2 minutes. Serve hot garnished with the freshly sliced spring onion.

Serves 4–6   Preparation time: 25 mins   Cooking time: 20 mins

Teochew Steamed Fish

1 whole pomfret or other white fish,
about 750 g–1 kg (1$^{1}/_{2}$–2 lbs),
or 4–6 fish fillets (about 1 kg/2 lbs)
$^{1}/_{4}$ cup (50 g) pickled mustard cabbage (*kiam chye*), soaked drained
and thinly sliced (see note)
1 medium tomato, cut into thin wedges
5 cm (2 in) fresh ginger, peeled and
thinly sliced
1 red finger-length chilli, deseeded
and thinly sliced lengthwise
3 or 4 salted plums (see note)
1 spring onion, cut into lengths
(optional)
2 dried black Chinese mushrooms,
soaked in water to soften, stems
discarded, caps sliced
$^{1}/_{4}$ cup (60 g) pork, very thinly sliced
(optional)

Seasonings
$^{1}/_{4}$ cup (60 ml) chicken stock or
$^{1}/_{4}$ teaspoon chicken stock granules
dissolved in $^{1}/_{4}$ cup (60 ml) hot water
1 tablespoon soy sauce
1 teaspoon Garlic Oil (page 31)
1 teaspoon rice wine
$^{1}/_{2}$ teaspoon sugar
$^{1}/_{4}$ teaspoon sesame oil

1 Clean the fish and pat it dry thoroughly. Mix the Seasonings in a large bowl until the sugar is completely dissolved. Add all the other ingredients to the bowl and mix well.
2 Place the fish on a plate or tray that fits inside a steamer or wok that can be covered. Spread the Seasoning mixture over the fish. Cover the steamer or wok and steam the fish over rapidly boiling water for 10 to 15 minutes until the fish is cooked. Do not overcook or the texture of the fish will be spoiled.

Note: Pickled mustard cabbage (*kiam chye*) is slightly sour and extremely salty. This heavily salted pickled cabbage needs to be soaked in fresh water for at least 15 minutes to remove some of the saltiness. **Salted plums** are lightly pickled in brine and sold in jars. They are sour and the seeds need to be removed before using. The Japanese version is called *umeboshi*.

Serves 4–6   Preparation time: 15 mins   Cooking time: 15 mins

Oyster Omelette   Orr Chien

8–10 large fresh oysters
1 tablespoon tapioca starch
$^{1}/_{2}$ tablespoon rice flour
4 tablespoons water
2 tablespoons oil
3 eggs, beaten
2 cloves garlic, minced
1 tablespoon rice wine
1 tablespoon soy sauce
Ground white pepper
Coriander leaves (cilantro), to garnish

Chilli Vinegar Dip
2 tablespoons rice vinegar
4 teaspoons chilli powder
4 teaspoons water
2 teaspoon soy sauce
$^{1}/_{2}$ teaspoon salt
$^{1}/_{2}$ teaspoon sugar

1 To make the Chilli Vinegar Dip, mix all the ingredients in a small bowl and set aside.
2 Rinse the oysters and drain well to get rid of any sand or grit. Combine the tapioca starch, rice flour and water in a bowl to make a thin batter.
3 Heat a wok or large skillet over high heat until very hot and add 1 tablespoon of the oil. Add the batter and cook for 15 seconds, then add the eggs and scramble with the batter. When the eggs are almost cooked, push all the ingredients to one side of the pan. Add the remaining oil and stir-fry the garlic for a few seconds, then mix everything together and stir-fry for 2 minutes. Add the rice wine, soy sauce, pepper and oysters, and continue to cook long enough to heat through, about 1 minute. Serve hot, garnished with fresh coriander leaves and dipping bowls of the Chilli Vinegar Dip on the side.

Note: Tapioca starch is made from ground tapioca root. It is used as a thickening agent for soups. Substitute cornflour.

Serves 4   Preparation time: 10 mins   Cooking time: 10 mins

Fish Head Curry

A cook who came to Singapore from the southwestern Indian state of Kerala, where this dish is unheard of, created Fish Head Curry back in the 1950s. Its popularity spread quickly and now there are dozens of different versions of this dish.

1 large fresh fish head (red snapper, threadfin or sea bream), about 1–1$\frac{1}{4}$ kg (2–2$\frac{1}{2}$ lbs), halved lengthwise and rinsed
2 heaped tablespoons tamarind pulp mashed with $\frac{1}{2}$ cup (125 ml) warm water, squeezed and strained for juice
10 small okra (about 150 g/5 oz total), stalks discarded
1 slender Asian eggplant (about 200 g/7 oz), cut into 6 pieces
2 tomatoes, cut into wedges
1 teaspoon salt
1 tablespoon sugar

Curry Sauce
2 stalks lemongrass, thick bottom third only, outer layers removed, inner part sliced
2$\frac{1}{2}$ cm (1 in) fresh turmeric root, peeled and sliced, or 1 teaspoon ground turmeric
5 cm (2 in) fresh ginger, peeled and sliced
10 red finger-length chillies, deseeded and sliced
20 shallots, peeled
10 cloves garlic, peeled
4 tablespoons oil
$\frac{1}{2}$ teaspoon brown mustard seeds
$\frac{1}{2}$ teaspoon fenugreek seeds
1 sprig curry leaves, rinsed
5 tablespoons fish curry powder or plain curry powder
2 cups (500 ml) water
2 cups (500 ml) thick coconut milk or 1 cup (250 ml) coconut cream mixed with 1 cup (250 ml) water
1 teaspoon salt

1 To prepare the Curry Sauce, grind the lemongrass, turmeric, ginger, chillies, shallots and garlic in a mortar or blender until fine, adding a little oil if necessary to keep the blades turning.
2 Heat the oil in a wok over medium high heat and stir-fry the mustard seeds until they pop, about 1 minute. Add the ground ingredients, fenugreek seeds and curry leaves, and stir-fry until fragrant, about 5 to 7 minutes. Add the curry powder and cook for another 2 minutes. Add 1 cup (250 ml) of the water and simmer for 2 minutes. Then add the remaining water, coconut milk and the fish head, season with the salt and bring to a boil.
3 Add the tamarind juice to the wok and continue to simmer, uncovered, until the fish is almost cooked, about 10 minutes. Add the okra and eggplant, and simmer until cooked, about 5 to 7 minutes. Add the tomatoes and season with the salt and sugar. Serve hot with freshly cooked white rice.

Note: If you've never eaten a fish head before, you might be a little cautious about trying it. Be assured that it adds a special sweetness and texture to the curry. The flesh, especially from the cheek pockets, is soft and delicious.

Serves 4–6   Preparation time: 25 mins   Cooking time: 30 mins

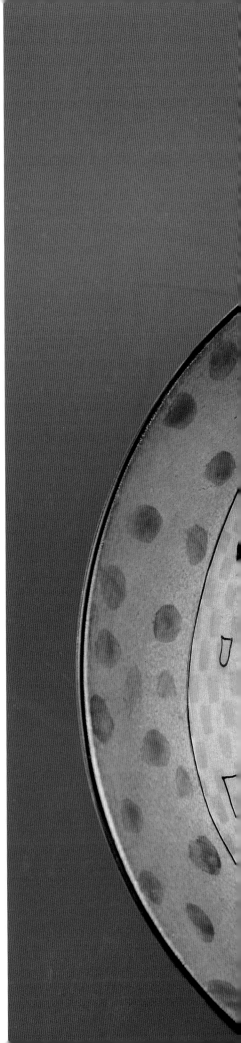

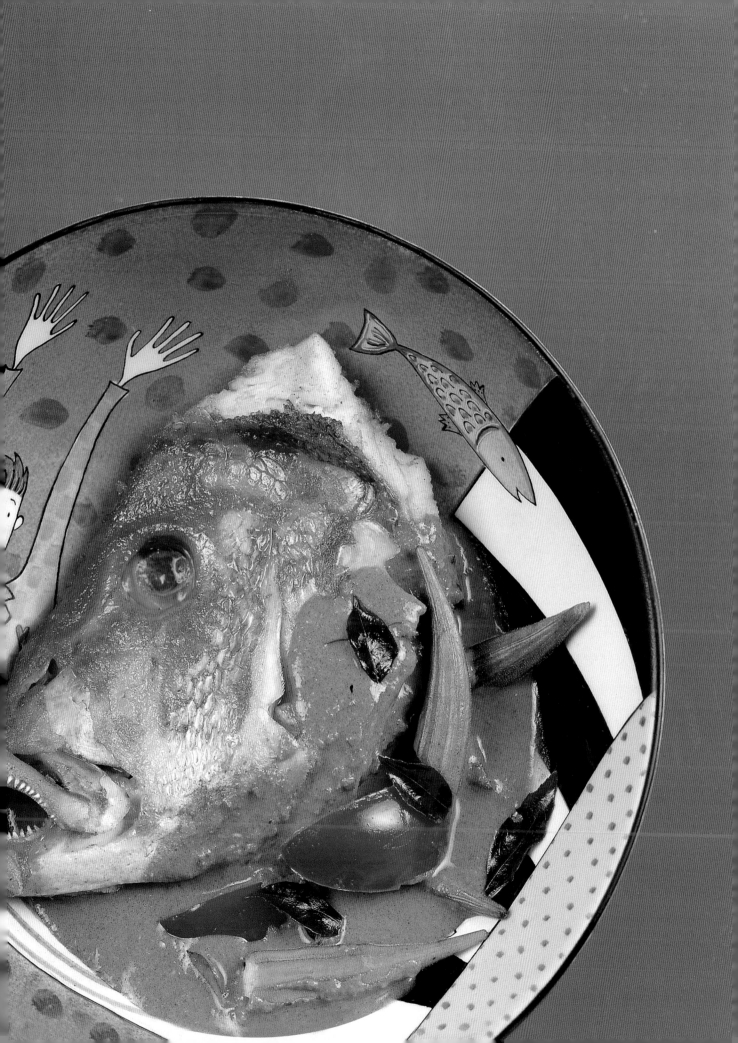

Barbecued Stingray   Ikan Pari Panggang

Stingray was an inexpensive and largely ignored fish until relatively recently, when this excellent way of cooking it—slathered with Chilli Sambal, wrapped in banana leaf and grilled over hot charcoal—filtered down from neighbouring Malaysia. Needless to say, the price of stingray has risen with the popularity of this dish. Any other firm white fish like swordfish or mahi-mahi may also be used with delicious results.

1 kg (2 lbs) stingray or any other firm white fish fillets, cut into 4 serving pieces
$1/4$ teaspoon salt
$1/2$ teaspoon white pepper
2 tablespoons fresh lime juice
2 large banana leaf sheets or aluminum foil (30 cm/12 in square)
Small limes (*limau kasturi*), halved, to serve

Chilli Sambal
5 red finger-length chillies, deseeded and sliced
3 *chili padi* (bird's-eye chillies), deseeded and sliced
3 cloves garlic, peeled
1 tablespoon oil
$1/2$ tablespoon tomato ketchup
$1/2$ tablespoon dried prawns, soaked to soften, then drained
1 tablespoon fresh lime juice
$1/4$ tablespoon sugar
Pinch of salt and freshly ground black pepper

1 To make the Chilli Sambal, grind the chillies and garlic to a paste in a mortar or blender, adding a little oil if necessary to keep the blades turning. Heat the oil in a wok over low heat and stir-fry the ground paste, tomato ketchup and dried prawns for 5 to 7 minutes. Add the lime juice, sugar, salt and pepper, and stir-fry until the sugar dissolves, about 2 minutes. Remove from the heat and set aside to cool.
2 Wash the stingray or fish fillets and pat dry with paper towels. Season with the salt, pepper and lime juice, and set aside to marinate for 15 to 20 minutes.
3 Soften the banana leaves by scalding them with boiling water in a tub or pot for 10 seconds. Drain the leaves and shake dry. Then spoon some Chilli Sambal onto each banana leaf (or aluminium foil sheet) and place 2 pieces of stingray or fish on each one. Spoon more Chilli Sambal on the stingray or fish and rub it into the flesh. Fold both sides of the banana leaves (or aluminium foil) over to form a packet and fasten with toothpicks.
4 Grill over a low charcoal fire or under a grill for 5 minutes on each side. To serve, place the package on a plate and open. Serve hot with limes halves on the side.

Note: Banana leaves give a special flavour and texture to food when cooking. An alternative is to wrap the fish in aluminum foil, although the flavour of the dish will not be quite the same.

Serves 4   Preparation time: 25 mins   Cooking time: 20 mins

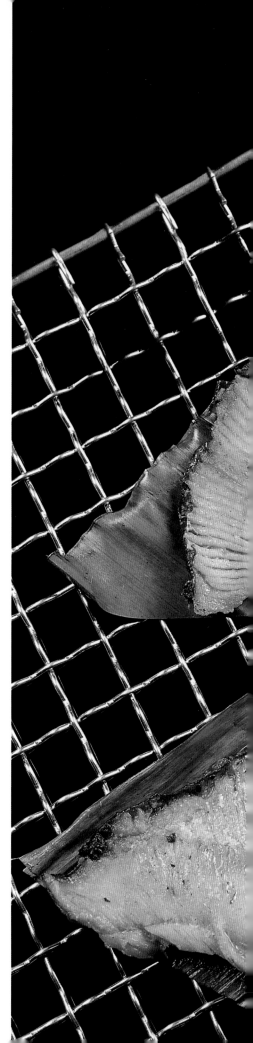

Deep-fried Baby Squid   Sotong Goreng

This sweet, crunchy Singaporean seafood creation has been embraced by generations of discerning local diners. It also makes an excellent appetiser or cocktail snack.

500 g (1 lb) baby squid (each about
    4–5 cm/1^1/$_2$–2 in long)
3 tablespoons cornstarch
1 egg, lightly beaten
Oil for deep-frying

Marinade
1 tablespoon soy sauce
2 teaspoons sugar
^{1}/$_2$ teaspoon sesame oil

Sauce
1 tablespoon oil
2 tablespoons honey
1 tablespoon bottled tomato ketchup
2 teaspoons each Worcestershire
    sauce, fresh lime juice, sweet bot-
    tled chilli sauce and soy sauce
^{1}/$_2$ teaspoon sesame oil
^{1}/$_2$ teaspoon black soy sauce
1 tablespoon cornstarch mixed with
    2 tablespoons water

1 Combine the Marinade ingredients in a bowl and mix to dissolve the sugar. Wash and dry the squid thoroughly, but do not remove the tentacles or skins. Season the squid with the Marinade and set aside to marinate while preparing the Sauce.

2 To make the Sauce, heat the oil in a wok or saucepan over medium heat and add all the Sauce ingredients, except the cornstarch. Stir to mix well and bring to a boil, then add the cornstarch and simmer over low heat, stirring, until the Sauce thickens and clears, about 1 to 2 minutes.

3 Dredge the marinated squid lightly in the cornstarch and dip into the egg. Heat the oil in a wok or large saucepan and deep-fry the squid until crispy and golden brown, about 3 to 5 minutes. Remove from the oil and set aside to drain. Then quickly toss the squid in the Sauce to coat well and serve while still hot.

Note: If baby squids are not available, substitute small fresh cuttlefish sliced thinly into ^{1}/$_2$ cm (^{1}/$_4$ in) rings.

Serves 6   Preparation time: 15 mins   Cooking time: 10 mins

Fried Fish with Spicy Prawn Sambal

1 kg (2 lbs) sole or other white fish
    fillets
^{1}/$_2$ teaspoon salt
^{1}/$_4$ teaspoon ground white pepper
Oil for deep-frying

Sauce
1 heaped tablespoon dried prawns,
    soaked in water to soften, drained
4 red finger-length chillies, deseeded
    and sliced
4 shallots, peeled
4 cloves garlic, peeled
2 tablespoons *belachan* (dried prawn
    paste), roasted (page 22)
1 stalk lemongrass, thick bottom
    third only, outer layers removed,
    inner part bruised
1 tablespoon sugar
2 tablespoons soy sauce
1 tablespoon sesame oil

1 Clean the fish thoroughly. Season with the salt and pepper and set aside.

2 To make the Sauce, grind the dried prawns, chillies, shallots, garlic and *belachan* to a paste in a mortar or blender, adding a little oil if necessary to keep the blades turning. Heat 1 tablespoon of the oil in a wok over low heat and gently stir-fry the ground paste, lemongrass and sugar for 5 minutes until the sugar is completely dissolved. Add the soy sauce and sesame oil, and stir to mix well. Remove the Sauce from the heat and set aside.

3 Heat the oil in a wok over high heat and once the oil is hot, deep-fry the seasoned fish fillets until light golden brown, about 3 to 5 minutes. Remove from the oil, drain and place on a platter. Drizzle the Sauce over the fish and serve hot, or serve the Sauce in a small bowl on the side.

Serves 4   Preparation time: 15 mins   Cooking time: 10 mins

Golden Prawns with Sweet Spicy Sauce

1 kg (2 lbs) large fresh prawns
2 tablespoons fresh lime juice
$1/_4$ teaspoon salt
$1/_4$ teaspoon pepper
Flour, for dusting
Oil for deep-frying
Carrot, shredded, to garnish
Cucumber, shredded, to garnish

Sweet Spicy Sauce
2 cm ($3/_4$ in) fresh galangal root,
  peeled and sliced
1 cm ($1/_2$ in) fresh ginger, peeled and
  sliced
3 shallots, peeled
5 cloves garlic, peeled
1 tablespoon oil
5–7 red finger-length chillies, deseeded and thinly sliced
5 tablespoons Palm Sugar Syrup
  (see note) or honey
4 heaped tablespoons (100 g)
  tamarind pulp mashed with 1 cup
  (250 ml) warm water, squeezed and
  strained for juice

1 Peel and devein the prawns, discarding the heads and shells. Place the prawns in a bowl, add the lime juice, salt and pepper, and mix well. Set aside for 10 minutes. Then rinse and pat dry with paper towels. Dust the prawns lightly with flour. Heat the oil in a wok and deep-fry the prawns for 1 to 2 minutes until golden. Remove from the oil and set aside to drain.

2 To make the Sweet Spicy Sauce, grind the galangal, ginger, shallots and garlic to a paste in a mortar or blender, adding a little oil if necessary to keep the blades turning. Heat the oil in a saucepan over medium heat and stir-fry the paste for 5 to 8 minutes, until fragrant. Add the remaining sauce ingredients, reduce the heat and simmer until it thickens, about 10 minutes. Remove from the heat and set aside to cool. When cooled, grind the sauce in a blender for a few seconds, then strain into a bowl.

3 Toss the prawns in the Sweet Spicy Sauce until well coated and serve with a mix of freshly shredded carrot and cucumber on the side.

Note: To prepare **Palm Sugar Syrup**, bring $1/_2$ cup (100 g) shaved palm sugar and $1/_2$ cup (125 ml) water to a boil in a small saucepan. Add a pandanus leaf or a drop of pandanus essence to the water, if desired. Then reduce the heat and simmer over low heat for 10 minutes until the liquid thickens and becomes syrupy. Strain, discard the pandanus leaf (if using).

Serves 4–6   Preparation time: 20 mins   Cooking time: 15 mins

Coconut Ginger Prawns with Lemongrass Curry

1 kg (2 lbs) large fresh prawns
$2^1/_2$ cm (1 in) fresh ginger, peeled
  and sliced into very thin shreds

Sauce
5 cm (2 in) fresh turmeric root,
  peeled and sliced, or 1 teaspoon
  ground turmeric
8 cm (3 in) fresh ginger, peeled and
  sliced
8 red finger-length chillies, deseeded
  and sliced
15 shallots, peeled
10 cloves garlic, peeled
2 tablespoons oil
3 stalks lemongrass, thick bottom
  third only, outer layers removed,
  inner part bruised
5 kaffir lime leaves
1 cup (250 ml) water
1 cup (250 ml) thick coconut milk or
  $1/_2$ cup (125 ml) coconut cream
  mixed with $1/_2$ cup (125 ml) water
$1/_2$ teaspoon salt
$1/_2$ teaspoon freshly ground black
  pepper

1 Remove the heads and shells from the prawns. Gently devein the prawns and set aside. Reserve the prawn heads and shells to make the Sauce.

2 To prepare the Sauce, grind the turmeric, ginger, chillies, shallots and garlic in a mortar or blender until fine, adding a little oil if necessary to keep the blades turning.

3 Heat the oil in a wok and stir-fry the ground paste with the reserved prawn heads and shells, lemongrass and lime leaves over medium heat for 5 to 7 minutes. When the prawn shells are pink, add the water and simmer for 5 minutes. Then add the coconut milk and bring to a boil. Reduce the heat and simmer, uncovered, over low heat for 10 minutes. Season with the salt and pepper.

4 Remove from the heat and strain the Sauce well. Discard the solids and return the Sauce to the pan. Add the prawns and shredded ginger, and simmer gently until the prawns are pink, about 5 minutes. Serve immediately with freshly cooked rice.

Serves 4–6   Preparation time: 25 mins   Cooking time: 25 mins

Tandoori Baked Fish   Macchi Tandoori

Tandoori chicken, marinated in an exotic blend of spices and roasted in a special clay oven or *tandoor*, is a North Indian classic that is very popular in Singapore. This version is prepared with fish, which goes very well with Cucumber Raita (see recipe below).

700 g (1$^1/_2$ lbs) white fish fillets
2 tablespoons fresh lemon juice
1 tablespoon ghee or melted butter, to baste
Lime or lemon, cut into wedges, to serve

Tandoori Paste
1 tablespoon coriander seeds
2 teaspoons cumin seeds
2 cm ($^3/_4$ in) fresh ginger, peeled and sliced
3 cloves garlic, peeled
3 red finger-length chillies, deseeded
$^1/_2$ cup (125 ml) plain yogurt
$^1/_4$ teaspoon sugar
$^1/_2$ teaspoon salt
$^1/_2$ teaspoon ground white pepper

1 Rub the fish fillets with the lemon juice and set aside.
2 To make the Tandoori Paste, dry-roast the coriander and cumin seeds in a skillet over low heat until fragrant, about 2 minutes. Set aside to cool. When cooled, grind the roasted seeds, ginger, garlic and chillies in a mortar or blender, adding a little yogurt if necessary to keep the blades turning. Add the yogurt and season with the sugar, salt and pepper. Mix well.
3 Rub the fish fillets with the Tandoori Paste and set aside to marinate for at least an hour.
4 Preheat the oven to 200°C (400°F). Place the fish on a rack with a baking tray directly below and bake in the oven for 15 to 20 minutes, basting from time to time with the ghee or melted butter. Serve hot with Cucumber Raita and lime or lemon wedges on the side.

Serves 4–6   Preparation time: 15 mins + marination time   Cooking time: 20 mins

Cucumber Raita   Cucumber in Yogurt Dressing

Raita, a soothing yogurt-based side dish, is an excellent foil to any spicy Indian dish. Although often made with a wide variety of vegetables and even bananas, Cucumber Raita is perhaps the most popular.

1 medium or 2 small cucumbers (about 300 g/10 oz total), peeled
$^1/_2$ tablespoon salt
2 shallots, peeled and very thinly sliced (optional)
$^1/_2$ cup (125 ml) plain yogurt
1 sprig mint leaves, coarsely chopped

1 Halve the cucumbers lengthwise and deseed them. Then cut crosswise into paper-thin slices. Sprinkle the salt over the cucumber and set aside to drain in a colander for 10 minutes. Squeeze out as much water from the cucumber as possible, then rinse off the salt and squeeze again. Allow to drain well.
2 Place the cucumber in a small bowl. Add the shallots, yogurt and mint leaves, and mix well. Serve chilled or at room temperature.

Note: Sprinkle a little chilli or ground cumin over the *raita* just before serving if desired.

Makes 1$^1/_2$ cups   Preparation time: 20 mins

Yu Sheng   Chinese New Year Raw Fish Salad

This refreshing dish tops the menu at every Chinese restaurant in Singapore during the 2-week Lunar New Year period. It is considered an auspicious dish as the term used for mixing the salad together sounds almost the same in Cantonese as the word symbolising good luck and prosperity (Lo Hei).

Salad
1 medium carrot, peeled
1 medium daikon radish, peeled
1 small yam, peeled, grated and
   deep-fried
$1/_2$ teaspoon each red and green food
   colouring (optional)
$1/_2$ cup (60 g) preserved sweet
   papaya or melon, sliced (see note)
$1/_2$ cup (60 g) pickled ginger, slivered
   (see note)
$1/_2$ cup (150 g) pomelo or grapefruit
   flesh, shredded by hand (see note)
$1/_2$ cup (50 g) prepared jellyfish,
   sliced (optional, see note)
4 kaffir lime leaves, slivered (optional)

Sauce
2 teaspoons sesame oil
5 tablespoons sweet Chinese plum
   sauce
3 tablespoons fresh lime juice

Fish Sashimi and Seasoning
150 g (5 oz) fresh salmon or other
   fish fillets, chilled and very thinly
   sliced
1 tablespoon Garlic Oil (page 31)
5 cm (2 in) young ginger, sliced into
   thin shreds
$1/_2$ teaspoon ground white pepper
1 tablespoon fresh lime juice

Garnishes
4 tablespoons coarsely crushed
   roasted peanuts
$1/_2$ tablespoon five spice powder
1 tablespoon white sesame seeds,
   dry-fried until golden
Flour Crisps (page 30)
Coriander leaves (cilantro), to garnish
   (optional)
2 small limes (*limau kasturi*), cut into
   wedges, to serve

1 Grate the carrot and radish into long, thin slices using a spiral slicer if available. Place them in separate mounds on a platter. Mix half of the yam slices with red food colouring and the other half with green food colouring, if desired, and place in separate mounds on the platter with the carrot and radish. Prepare the rest of the Salad and place separately on the platter.
2 Mix all the Sauce ingredients together and set aside in a small bowl.
3 To serve, place everything on the dining table: the platter of Salad, a plate of the raw fish, small bowls of the fish seasoning next to it and a plate of Garnishes. Start with the Fish Sashimi and Seasoning—toss the raw fish in the seasoning and place it on the platter with the Salad. Pour the Sauce over and sprinkle the Garnishes, except the lime halves, over it. Then, diners can help to mix the salad with chopsticks to ensure good luck. Serve with the lime wedges on the side.

Note: Preserved sweet papaya or melon are candied slices of the fruits that are coated with sugar. They are sold in Chinese grocery stores. Pickled ginger are thin slices of young ginger that are pickled in salt, and then in vinegar. They are sold in most supermarkets or Asian stores. Pomelo is a citrus fruit that is larger than grapefruit but not as juicy. Prepared jellyfish are sold in ready-to-eat packets.

Serves 4–6   Preparation time: 60 mins

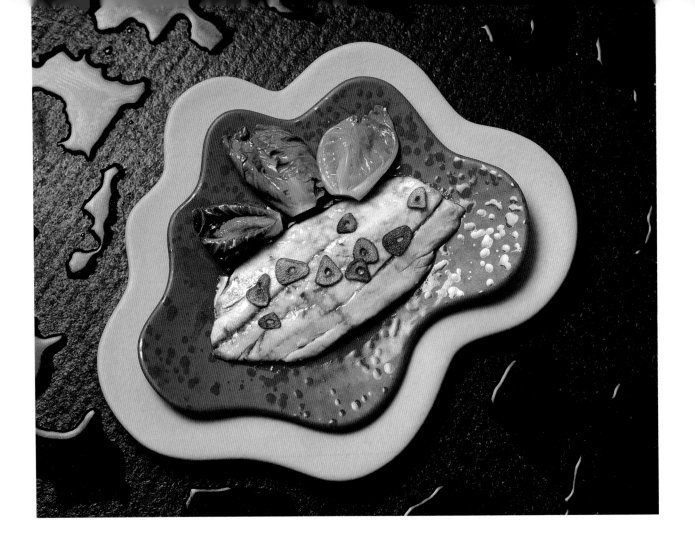

Steamed Fish with Vinegar Soy Dressing

Creative Singapore cooks do not hesitate to experiment with new recipes. Here is an extremely healthy local Chinese version of a Western steamed fish fillet with vegetables.

500 g (1 lb) seabass or cod fillet,
  sliced into thin steaks
1/4 teaspoon salt
1/4 teaspoon pepper
2 teaspoons oil
3–4 cloves garlic, sliced
350 g (12 oz) baby *kailan* (Chinese
  broccoli or kale), briefly blanched in
  boiling water
1 tablespoon soy sauce
1/2 teaspoon sesame oil
1 1/2 tablespoons black Chinese rice
  vinegar or balsamic vinegar

1 Season the fish lightly on both sides with the salt and pepper. Place the fish on a plate and steam in a wok or steamer for 6 to 8 minutes.
2 While the fish is steaming, heat the oil in a small skillet and stir-fry the garlic over medium heat for 1 to 2 minutes until browned. Remove the garlic and place on paper towels to drain. Add the baby *kailan* to the wok and stir-fry until the leaves have wilted slightly but are still crunchy, about 1 to 2 minutes. Remove from the heat and set aside.
3 Heat the soy sauce, sesame oil and vinegar in a small saucepan over low heat for 1 minute and set aside.
4 When the fish is cooked, remove it from the steamer and place onto individual serving plates. Drizzle the vinegar sauce over the fish and garnish with a sprinkling of the reserved garlic. Serve hot with the baby *kailan* on the side.

Note: Balsamic vinegar is a mild, dark brown vinegar with a sweet-sour flavour. It is made from reduced grape juice that was aged in wooden casks. It makes a wonderfully light vinaigrette for salads and other foods. Available bottled in supermarkets and well-stocked provision shops.

Serves 4   Preparation time: 15 mins   Cooking time: 20 mins

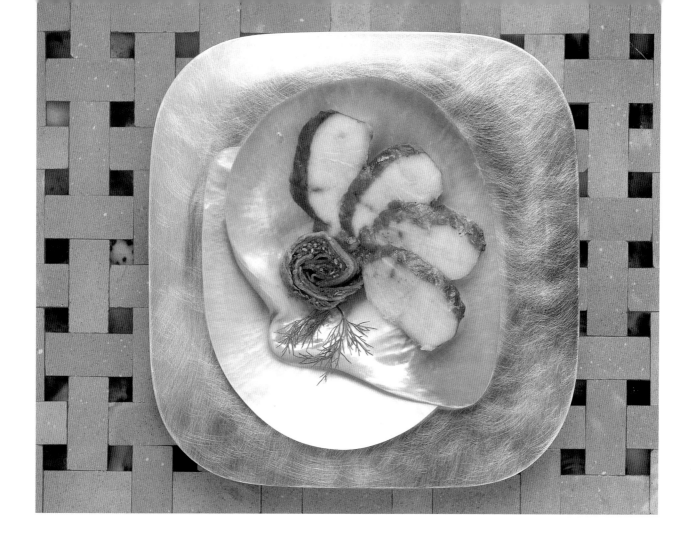

Tea-smoked Fish Fillets

Smoking food—especially duck or pork—over a mixture of tea leaves is a popular method of preparing and preserving food in the western Yunnan and Sichuan provinces of China. This excellent Singapore adaptation makes use of the abundant supply of local seafood.

600 g (1¹/₄ lbs) seabass or other firm
  white fish fillet like snapper or garoupa
Fennel sprigs, to garnish (optional)
Pickled mustard cabbage (*kiam chye*)

Marinade
¹/₂ cup (125 ml) ice water
¹/₄ cup (60 ml) ginger juice (see note)
5 tablespoons soy sauce
1 tablespoon sugar
1 tablespoon salt

Smoking Mix
20 cloves
5 star anise pods
5 cloves garlic, peeled and crushed
3 cinnamon sticks (each 8 cm/3 in)
5 tablespoons Chinese black tea leaves
5 tablespoons uncooked rice

1 Combine the Marinade ingredients in a bowl until the salt and sugar are completely dissolved. Drizzle the Marinade over the fish fillet and set aside for 3 hours. Then drain the fish, pat dry with paper towels and set aside.
2 Heat a wok over low heat and add the Smoking Mix. Place the fish on a wire grill or round bamboo rack inside the wok at least 5 cm (2 in) above the Smoking Mix. Cover the wok and allow to smoke over low heat for 10 to 15 minutes until the fish takes on a light brown colour and is cooked through.
3 Cut the fish into serving slices, garnish with fennel sprigs, if using, and serve either hot or cold with pickled mustard cabbage on the side.

Note: To make the ginger juice, grate 8 cm (4 in) young ginger to make ¹/₂ cup of grated ginger. Mix with 2 tablespoons water, then strain the mixture through a fine sieve, pressing with the back of a spoon, to obtain ¹/₄ cup (60 ml) of juice. If using a grill or charcoal fire, allow the charcoal to burn down to the red embers, then add the Smoking Mix, place the fish on the grill, cover and cook until done.

Serves 4   Preparation time: 20 mins + marination time   Cooking time: 15 mins

Claypot Rice

A simple Cantonese one-pot dish, in which rice is cooked in a claypot with succulent chunks of chicken, fragrant Chinese sausage, black mushrooms and seasonings. The Chinese believe that a claypot is essential to ensure the correct flavour and fragrance of this dish, though any other type of covered earthenware container could be used.

500 g (1 lb) boneless chicken meat, cut into bite-sized chunks
6 dried black Chinese mushrooms, soaked to soften, stems discarded,
  caps quartered
1 tablespoon oil
2 cups (400 g) uncooked long-grain rice, washed and drained
$1^1/_2$ cups (375 ml) chicken stock or $^1/_2$ teaspoon chicken stock granules
  dissolved in $1^1/_2$ cups (375 ml) hot water
1 sweet dried Chinese sausage (*lap cheong*), sliced
4 cm ($1^1/_2$ in) fresh ginger, peeled and thinly sliced
1 spring onion, thinly sliced, to garnish (optional)

Marinade
1 tablespoon oil
3 tablespoons oyster sauce
1 tablespoon rice wine
1 tablespoon soy sauce
1 teaspoon black soy sauce
1 teaspoon sugar
$^1/_2$ teaspoon sesame oil
$^1/_2$ teaspoon ground white pepper
$^1/_2$ tablespoon cornstarch

1 Combine the Marinade ingredients in a small bowl and pour over the chicken and mushrooms, and mix to coat them well. Set the chicken and mushrooms aside to marinate for at least 2 to 4 hours.
2 Heat the oil in a large seasoned claypot over high heat and stir-fry the drained rice for 2 minutes in the oil until lightly browned. Add the chicken stock, bring to a boil, then reduce the heat and simmer, covered, over low heat for 15 minutes.
3 Spread the marinated chicken and mushrooms, sausage and ginger on top of the rice. Cover again and cook for another 10 minutes. Remove from the heat, garnish with freshly sliced spring onion and serve.

Note: Claypots are the Chinese version of a casserole dish. While claypots are cooked on the stovetop, casseroles are usually bound for the oven. The design of the claypot ensures that food stays piping hot even if the meal is delayed. To season a new claypot, immerse it completely in water for 24 hours, or see package instructions.

Serves 4   Preparation time: 15 mins + marination time   Cooking time: 30 mins

Sweet Pork Ribs Wrapped in Fragrant Pandanus Leaves

The elusive fragrance of pandanus leaves permeates a number of rice, meat and chicken dishes of Malay or Nonya origin, while pandanus essence extracted from the leaves is often used in cakes and desserts. The use of pandanus to wrap foods (most often seasoned chicken) before deep-frying is borrowed quite recently from Thailand. This Singapore adaptation uses pork ribs.

3 shallots, peeled
5 cloves garlic, peeled
3 tablespoons Worcestershire sauce (see note)
2 tablespoons sweet plum sauce or honey (see note)
$1^1/_2$ tablespoons steak sauce (see note)
1 tablespoon hoisin sauce
$^1/_2$–1 teaspoon five spice powder
4 tablespoons oil
1 teaspoon sesame oil
700 g ($1^1/_2$ lbs) meaty pork ribs or chicken thighs, cut into serving pieces
24 pandanus leaves, rinsed and dried
Oil for deep-frying

1 Grind the shallots and garlic in a mortar and mix with all other ingredients, except the meat, pandanus leaves and oil for deep-frying. Rub this mixture into the meat and set aside to marinate for 2 hours.
2 Wrap each piece of pork rib or chicken thigh in a pandanus leaf, tying it in a simple knot so the meat is enclosed by the leaf as shown.
3 Deep-fry the meat parcels in very hot oil for 3 to 5 minutes until cooked. Serve hot, still in the pandanus leaf, allowing each diner to unwrap his or her own portions.

Note: If unavailable, substitute pandanus leaves with parchment paper. Wrap the ribs envelope-style and fasten with a staple before frying. Worcestershire sauce and steak sauce are both of English origin, and are available in supermarkets. Sweet plum sauce is available where Chinese foods are sold.

Serves 4   Preparation time: 20 mins + marination time   Cooking time: 10 mins

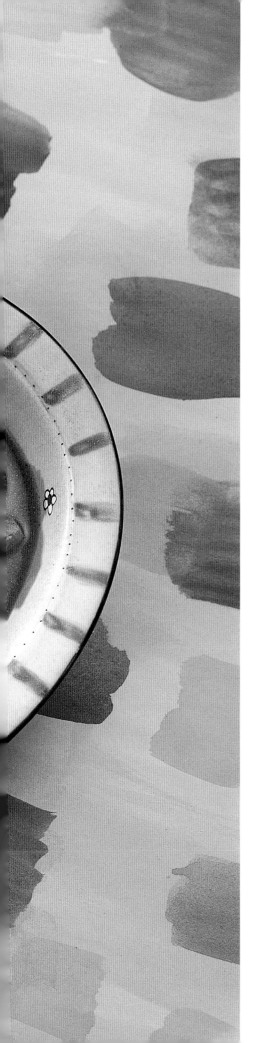

Indian Mutton Soup   Sup Kambing

Also known as Sup Tulang or Bone Soup, this robust dish is one of the more popular hawker dishes in Singapore. It makes a great late-night meal or luncheon served with lots of crusty French bread to soak up the soup.

5 cm (2 in) fresh ginger, peeled and sliced
6 cloves garlic, peeled
1 kg (2 lbs) meaty mutton or lamb ribs
1 onion, sliced or 5 shallots, sliced
1 heaped tablespoon ground coriander
1 teaspoon ground fennel
1 teaspoon ground cumin
$1/2$ teaspoon ground turmeric
$1^1/2$ teaspoons salt
1 teaspoon freshly ground black pepper
8–12 cups (2–3 litres) water
$1/2$ tablespoon oil
2 leeks, white part only, sliced (optional)
5 cardamom pods, bruised
3 star anise pods
1 cinnamon stick
1 tomato, cut into wedges
Crispy Fried Shallots, to garnish (page 31)
Chinese celery or coriander leaves (cilantro), coarsely chopped, to garnish

1 Grind the ginger and garlic together in a mortar to a paste. Place the paste in a pot with the mutton or lamb ribs, onion, coriander, fennel, cumin and turmeric powders. Season with the salt and pepper. Add 12 cups (3 litres) of water if using mutton, but only 8 cups (2 litres) if using lamb, which will cook more quickly. Simmer over medium heat, uncovered, until the meat is soft, about $1^1/2$ hours for mutton and 1 hour for lamb.
2 Heat the oil in a skillet over medium heat and stir-fry the leeks, cardamom, star anise and cinnamon until the leeks are tender, about 5 minutes.
3 Add the fried mixture to the mutton soup and simmer for another 2 minutes. Then add the tomato and stir to mix well. Serve garnished with Crispy Fried Shallots and Chinese celery leaves, and crusty French bread on the side.

Serves 4–6   Preparation time: 15 mins   Cooking time: 1 hour 40 mins

Chicken in Coconut Curry   Ayam Lemak

A wonderfully fragrant Malay dish that uses fresh aromatic roots and herbs to create an enticing flavour. If you don't like your food fiery hot, omit or reduce the amount of chillies called for in this recipe.

1 fresh chicken (about 1 kg/2 lbs), washed and cut into serving pieces
2 cups (500 ml) water
3 cups (750 ml) thick coconut milk or 1$^1/_2$ cups (375 ml) coconut cream mixed with 1$^1/_2$ cups (375 ml) water
1 teaspoon salt
$^1/_2$ teaspoon ground white pepper
3–5 finger-length chillies, halved lengthwise and deseeded
5–10 red or green *chilli padi* (bird's-eye chillies), left whole (optional)
Crispy Fried Shallots (page 31), to garnish (optional)

Spice Mix
2$^1/_2$ cm (1 in) fresh turmeric root, peeled and sliced, or 1 teaspoon ground turmeric
2$^1/_2$ cm (1 in) fresh ginger, peeled and sliced
5 red finger-length chillies, deseeded and sliced
10 shallots, peeled
8 cloves garlic, peeled
3 tablespoons oil
2 stalks lemongrass, thick bottom third only, outer layers removed, inner part bruised
2$^1/_2$ cm (1 in) fresh galangal root, peeled and sliced
5 kaffir lime leaves
1 teaspoon ground coriander

1 Pat the chicken dry with paper towels and set aside.
2 To make the Spice Mix, grind the turmeric, ginger, chillies, shallots and garlic to a paste in a mortar or blender, adding a little oil if necessary to keep the blades turning. Heat the oil in a wok over medium to high heat, add the ground paste, lemongrass, galangal, lime leaves and ground coriander. Then reduce the heat to medium and stir-fry for 5 to 7 minutes until fragrant.
3 Add the chicken and stir-fry until all the pieces are coated with the spices, about 1 minute. Then add the water, increase to medium high heat and simmer, uncovered, until the chicken is half cooked, about 15 minutes.
4 Add the coconut milk and season with the salt and pepper. Continue to simmer over medium to high heat for another 25 minutes. Then add the chillies and cook until the meat is tender, another 10 minutes. Serve hot, garnished with the Crispy Fried Shallots if using.

Serves 4–6   Preparation time: 30 mins   Cooking time: 55 mins

Duck Braised in Fragrant Soy

A Teochew recipe usually made with goose, this simple but tasty method of braising in soy flavoured with cinnamon, star anise and cloves works equally well with duck or chicken.

1 fresh duck (about 2 kg/4 lbs)
1 teaspoon five spice powder
10 cloves garlic, crushed
3 tablespoons black soy sauce
$^1/_2$ tablespoon oil
2 tablespoons sugar
10 shallots, peeled and lightly bruised
5 cm (2 in) fresh galangal or ginger root, peeled and bruised
5 cinnamon sticks
15 star anise pods
20 cloves
$^1/_2$ cup (125 ml) soy sauce
16 cups (4 litres) water

Garlic and Vinegar Sauce
5 cloves garlic, minced
1 finger-length chilli, deseeded and minced (optional)
4 tablespoons rice vinegar or white vinegar

1 To prepare the Garlic and Vinegar Sauce, mix all the ingredients a bowl and set aside.
2 Bring a kettle of water to a boil. Clean the duck and remove as much fat as possible. Scald the outside of the duck with hot water to remove the remaining wax and fat, then set it aside to drain. Rub the duck inside and out with the five spice powder, crushed garlic and black soy sauce.
3 Place the oil in a big pot, add the sugar and heat over low heat until the sugar caramelises, about 10 minutes. Add the shallots and galangal, and stir to mix well. Then add the cinnamon, star anise, cloves and stir again. Add the soy sauce and water, increase the heat to high and bring to a boil.
4 Add the duck with its seasonings, and simmer, covered, over low heat for $1^1/_2$ hours. Remove the cover and simmer for another 30 minutes. Add more water if needed. Remove the duck from the pot and set aside to cool. Strain the sauce into a saucepan and discard the solids. Skim the fat from the sauce, then simmer until it reduces to a gravy.
5 Debone the duck and cut into serving slices. Serve with small bowls of the Garlic and Vinegar Sauce and warm gravy on the side.

Serves 6–8   Preparation time: 30 mins   Cooking time: 2 hours 20 mins

Bak Kut Teh   Pork Rib Soup

A popular late-night or early morning pick-me-up, this flavourful soup can be prepared with various cuts of meat, although this version using ribs is most popular.

500 g (1 lb) pork ribs, cleaned, separated and cut into lengths
One 150-g (5-oz) piece lean pork
1 bulb garlic, unpeeled, washed
12 cups (3 litres) water
4 tablespoons black soy sauce
2 tablespoons soy sauce
2 teaspoons sugar
1 red finger-length chilli, thinly sliced, to serve (optional)
Black soy sauce, to serve (optional)

Seasoning
1 packet of Bak Kut Teh Spices (see note), a combination of cloves, star anise, cinnamon, rock sugar and various Chinese medicinal herbs (*gan cao*, *luo han guo*, *dang xin*, *chuan kong*, *dang guei* and *sheng di*)

1 Place the pork ribs, pork and garlic with the water in a large pot. Wrap the Seasonings in a piece of clean cheesecloth and add to the pan. Add the soy sauces and sugar, and bring to a boil. Then reduce the heat to low and simmer gently, covered, for 1$^1/_2$ to 2 hours, until the meat is very tender and almost falling off the bones. Discard the cheesecloth filled with the Seasonings.
2 To serve, slice the pork meat into small pieces. Place a few pieces of meat in individual serving bowls with a few ribs and whole cloves of garlic, and ladle the hot stock over the meat. Serve with a small bowl of sliced fresh red chilli in black soy sauce on the side. Serve immediately.

Note: Packets of Bak Kut Teh Spices are sold in supermarkets and food shops in Singapore, Malaysia and Australia. You can also stop by a Chinese medicine shop and ask for seasonings to make Bak Kut Teh.

Yields 6 cups   Preparation time: 15 mins   Cooking time: 1 hour 45 mins

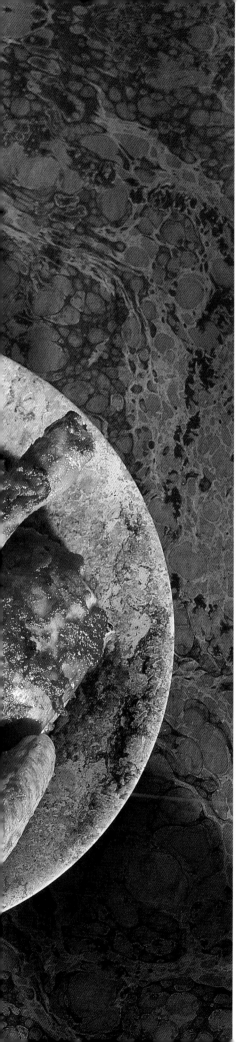

Ayam Panggang Barbecued Spicy Chicken

Barbecuing was very common among Malay cooks in the old days when every *dapur* (kitchen) had a wood fire. These days, barbecued or *panggang* foods are more likely to be found at food stalls, where whole chickens are generally replaced with chicken wings or drumsticks.

1 whole chicken (about 1 kg/2 lbs), quartered or cut into serving pieces, or 6 chicken legs

Marinade
2 cloves garlic, peeled
$2^1/_2$ cm (1 in) fresh ginger, peeled and sliced
1 tablespoon fresh lime juice
$^1/_2$ teaspoon salt

Barbecue Chilli Paste
2 *chili padi* (bird's-eye chillies), deseeded and sliced (optional)
6 shallots, peeled
3 cloves garlic, peeled
1 ripe tomato
5 red finger-length chillies, deseeded and sliced
1 tablespoon oil
1 tablespoon fresh lime juice
2 teaspoons sugar
$^1/_4$ teaspoon salt
$^1/_4$ teaspoon pepper

1 To prepare the Marinade, grind the garlic and ginger together in a mortar. Mix this paste with the lime juice and salt, then rub the mixture into the chicken pieces. Set the seasoned chicken aside to marinate for 30 minutes.
2 To prepare the Barbecue Chilli Paste, steam or blanch the *chili padi*, shallots, garlic and tomato for 5 minutes in a saucepan with a bit of water. Then set the steamed ingredients aside to cool. Place the red chillies and the cooled ingredients into a blender and grind to a coarse paste.
3 Heat the oil in a pan and stir-fry the ground ingredients over low heat for 5 minutes until fragrant. Season with the lime juice, sugar, salt and pepper, and cook for another 5 minutes.
4 Grill the marinated chicken over a charcoal fire or under a broiler for 2 to 3 minutes on each side. Remove from the heat and rub the chicken thoroughly with the cooked Barbecue Chilli Paste and set aside for at least 10 minutes to allow the flavours to penetrate.
5 Return the chicken to the fire and grill until tender and golden brown on both sides, another 2 to 3 minutes on each side. Serve hot.

Note: The Barbecue Chilli Paste can be prepared several hours in advance. It is a very versatile paste that can also be used to season beef or seafood.

Serves 4   Preparation time: 25 mins   Cooking time: 40 mins

Buntut Asam Pedas   Spicy Oxtail Stew with Tamarind

Oxtail has long been a popular Singapore dish, prepared almost as an English-style stew by Hainanese cooks. This is a simple, delicious recipe, richly flavoured with the silky texture of oxtail enhanced by Malay or Indonesian spices.

1 kg (2 lbs) oxtail, fat trimmed off and
  cut into serving pieces
8–10 cups (2–2$^1/_2$ litres) water
$^1/_2$ teaspoon salt or more to taste
$^1/_2$ teaspoon pepper
Crispy Fried Shallots (page 31),
  to garnish (optional)

Marinade
2$^1/_2$ cm (1 in) fresh turmeric root,
  peeled and sliced, or 1 teaspoon
  ground turmeric
4 cm (1$^1/_2$ in) fresh galangal root,
  peeled and sliced
10–12 red finger-length chillies,
  deseeded and sliced
5–10 *chili padi* (bird's-eye chillies),
  deseeded and sliced (optional)
10 shallots, peeled
8 cloves garlic, peeled
2 stalks lemongrass, thick bottom
  third only, outer layers removed,
  inner part sliced
$^1/_2$ cup (125 ml) water
$^1/_2$ cup (150 g) tamarind pulp, mashed
  with 1$^1/_2$ cups (375 ml) warm water,
  squeezed and strained for juice
5 kaffir lime leaves, very thinly sliced
3 tablespoons tomato paste or
  5 tablespoons tomato ketchup
1 tablespoon sugar (if using tomato
  ketchup, omit this)

1 To make the Marinade, grind the turmeric, galangal, chillies, shallots, garlic and lemongrass in a mortar or blender until smooth, adding a little water if necessary to keep the blades turning. Combine the ground mixture with the rest of the Marinade ingredients. Rub the Marinade into the oxtail and set aside to marinate for at least 2 hours or overnight.

2 Bring the water to a boil in a pot. Add the marinated oxtail, reduce the heat and simmer, covered, over low heat for 30 minutes. Then simmer, uncovered, for another 30 minutes until the oxtail is tender and the broth is reduced by half. Stir periodically to prevent the meat from burning and add more water if the broth evaporates too quickly.

3 Season with the salt and pepper and garnish with Crispy Fried Shallots. Serve hot with freshly steamed rice.

Serves 4–6   Preparation time: 20 mins + marination time   Cooking time: 1 hour

Indian Mutton Curry   Kambing Korma

1 kg (2 lbs) mutton or lamb, cubed
9 cups (2^1/$_4$ litres) water
5 cm (2 in) fresh ginger, sliced
10 green finger-length chillies, deseeded
10 shallots, peeled
10 cloves garlic, peeled
3 tablespoons oil
4 large onions, peeled and sliced
6 cardamom pods, bruised
5 candlenuts or 20 raw cashew nuts,
   ground
5 star anise pods
4 cinnamon sticks
6 tablespoons meat curry powder
1 sprig curry leaves
3 potatoes, peeled and cubed
1 cup (250 ml) plain yogurt
1^1/$_2$ teaspoons salt
1 tablespoon ground white pepper
2 tablespoons tamarind pulp mashed
   with 4 tablespoons warm water,
   squeezed and strained for juice
4–6 green finger-length chillies, halved
   lengthwise and deseeded
6 small tomatoes, quartered (optional)

1 Cover the mutton with 8 cups (2 liters) water in a pot. Grind the ginger, chillies, shallots and garlic in a mortar or blender, adding 1 cup (250 ml) of water to keep the blades turning. Add the ground mixture to the pot and bring to a boil. Reduce the heat and simmer, uncovered, until the meat is tender, about 1^1/$_2$ hours for mutton and 1 hour for lamb.

2 Heat the oil in a skillet and stir-fry the onions for 3 minutes. Add the cardamom pods, candlenuts or cashew nuts, star anise, cinnamon, curry powder and curry leaves and stir-fry for 5 minutes until fragrant. Remove from the heat and add the fried mixture to the pot with the mutton.

3 Add the potatoes, yogurt, salt, pepper and tamarind juice, and continue to simmer until the meat is soft and cooked through, about 20 to 30 minutes. Add the green chillies and tomatoes if using and stir. Serve immediately with freshly cooked white rice.

Serves 6–8   Preparation time: 30 mins   Cooking time: 1^1/$_2$–2^1/$_2$ hours

Roast Duck and Rock Melon

1 ripe rock melon or cantaloupe
1 fresh duck (about 2 kg/4 lbs)
4 tablespoons Chinese plum sauce
3 tablespoons oil
1 teaspoon sesame oil

Seasonings
4 star anise pods
1 cinnamon stick
2 tablespoons black bean paste (*tau cheo*), mashed
2 tablespoons sweet black sauce
1 tablespoon soy sauce
$1/2$ teaspoon black soy sauce
1 tablespoon sugar
1 teaspoon sesame oil

Blanching Liquid
8 cups (2 litres) water
1 cup (250 ml) Chinese red vinegar (see note) or white vinegar
1 cup (250 ml) rice wine
2 large limes or lemons, sliced
3 tablespoons sugar syrup

1 Halve and deseed the melon. Use a small melon baller to scoop out 1 cup of the flesh. Place the melon balls in a bowl and set aside. Then peel and purée the rest of the melon and reserve 1 cup (250 ml) of the juice for the Sauce.
2 Wash and pat the duck dry. Mix all the Seasonings in a bowl and pour into the duck cavity. Seal the duck cavity at both ends with satay sticks or small skewers.
3 Pour the Blanching Liquid ingredients into a large pot and bring to a boil. Hold the duck firmly with one hand suspended over the pot and use a ladle to pour the hot liquid over the duck repeatedly for a minute with the other hand. Using a S-hook, hang the duck up in an airy space or under the sun for at least 2 hours for the skin to dry thoroughly. Roast the duck in a pre-heated oven at 200°C (400°F) for 45 minutes. Set aside to cool, then debone and cut into serving slices.
4 To make a sauce, combine the reserved melon juice, plum sauce, sesame oil and oil in a small bowl. Arrange the duck slices and melon balls on a plate and drizzle the sauce over or serve the sauce in a small bowl on the side.

Note: To save time, you can buy red-roasted Chinese duck from a Chinese BBQ shop. There are two types of Chinese vinegar, one almost black (often referred to as Tientsin vinegar) and the other a light reddish brown. The flavour is quite different, so try to find the latter for this dish.

Serves 6–8   Preparation time: 30 mins   Cooking time: 45 mins

Stuffed Yam Croquettes   Wu Kok

A Teochew delicacy, these croquettes are filled with bits of Char Siew (Barbecued Pork). You may be able to pick up some Char Siew from a Chinese store or the market.

1 kg (2 lbs) yams or sweet potatoes
1/2 cup (75 g) tapioca starch or cornstarch
1/2 cup (125 ml) vegetable shortening or pork oil (see note)
1/2 teaspoon five spice powder
1 teaspoon sesame oil
1 teaspoon salt
1 tablespoon sugar
1/2 teaspoon ground white pepper
Oil for deep-frying
Sweet bottled chilli sauce, to serve

Filling
1 small onion, diced
1 small carrot, diced
1/3 cup (50 g) fresh or frozen green peas
1 tablespoon oyster sauce
1 tablespoon soy sauce
1 tablespoon cornstarch
1/2 teaspoon sesame oil
1/2 teaspoon five spice powder
1/2 teaspoon sugar

Char Siew (Barbecued Pork)
200 g (7 oz) pork loin, cut into a long thick strip
2 tablespoons sugar
1 1/2 tablespoons soy sauce
2 teaspoons black soy sauce
1/2 teaspoon five spice powder
1/2 teaspoon sesame oil
1/2 teaspoon rice wine

1 First prepare the Char Siew by mixing the pork with all the ingredients and setting aside to marinate for 1 hour. Then drain the meat and roast on a wire rack over a roasting pan in a preheated oven at 200°C (400°F) for 30 minutes. Remove from the oven and set aside to cool. Then dice the meat.
2 To make the Filling, mix the Filling ingredients with the diced Char Siew in a bowl. Cover and set aside to chill in the refrigerator.
3 Peel the yam or sweet potatoes and cut the flesh into small chunks. Steam for 30 minutes over boiling water until soft. Mash the cooked yam or sweet potatoes in a small bowl and set aside.
4 Mix the tapioca starch with 3 to 4 tablespoons boiling water to form a smooth dough. Add the vegetable shortening or pork oil, five spice powder, sesame oil, salt, sugar, pepper and the mashed yam, and mix thoroughly. Divide the mixture into 20 equal portions and shape each portion into a ball.
5 Divide the Filling into 20 portions. Flatten each portion of the yam mixture and place a portion of the Filling in it. Shape the mixture around the Filling to enclose it and form a dumpling. Repeat with the rest of the yam mixture and Filling to form 20 yam dumplings in all.
6 Deep-fry the yam dumplings over moderate heat in a wok or deep-fryer until light golden brown, about 7 minutes. Remove from the heat and set aside to drain. Serve hot with a small bowl of sweet bottled chilli sauce on the side.

Note: Traditionally, this dish is made using pork oil. Pork oil or lard is made by chopping hard (back) pork fat into small pieces and cooking over low heat with 2 tablespoons water until the water evaporates and all the oil runs out.

Makes 20 yam croquettes   Preparation time: 55 mins + marination time
Cooking time: 1 hour 20 mins

Chicken Braised in Soy

The ingredients and seasonings are typically Chinese, but the final treatment of this dish shows an innovative approach, baking the chicken in individual potato moulds which makes a lovely presentation. The chicken can be cooked in advance and the dish completed by preparing the potatoes and baking the assembled dish in the oven just before serving.

1 whole chicken (about 1 kg/2 lbs), cut into small pieces
Oil for deep-frying
12 dried black Chinese mushrooms, soaked in warm water to soften, stems discarded, caps quartered
10 button mushrooms, halved
1 tablespoon butter
3 large potatoes, peeled and thinly sliced lengthwise

Marinade
1 egg, lightly beaten
2 tablespoons soy sauce
1 tablespoon oyster sauce
$1/_2$ tablespoon black soy sauce
$1/_2$ teaspoon pepper

Sauce
1 tablespoon oil
5 cloves garlic, minced
3 star anise pods
1 cinnamon stick
6 cm ($2^1/_2$ in) fresh ginger, peeled and sliced
4 tablespoons rice wine
2 tablespoons soy sauce
1 tablespoon black soy sauce
1 tablespoon oyster sauce
2 teaspoons sugar
1 teaspoon sesame oil
$1/_2$ teaspoon five spice powder
2 teaspoons cornstarch mixed with 2 tablespoons water

1 Combine the Marinade ingredients in a bowl. Rub the Marinade into the chicken and set aside to marinate for 10 minutes. Then pat the chicken dry and deep-fry in very hot oil until half cooked, about 3 minutes.

2 To prepare the Sauce, heat the oil in a wok or pot over high heat and stir-fry the garlic, star anise and cinnamon for 1 minute. Add the deep-fried chicken, both types of mushrooms and ginger and stir-fry for 3 minutes. Then add the remaining Sauce ingredients, except the cornstarch, and simmer for 2 minutes. Add the cornstarch mixture and stir to thicken the Sauce, about 5 minutes. Remove from the heat and set aside to cool.

3 Preheat the oven to 200°C (400°F). In a saucepan, heat the butter with 1 teaspoon oil and sauté the thinly sliced potatoes until half cooked.

4 Line 4 to 6 ovenproof bowls with the half-cooked potatoes, ensuring that they overlap. Fill the bowls with the chicken mixture and cover with the remaining potato slices. Bake in the oven for 5 to 7 minutes until the potatoes are golden brown.

5 To serve, unmould the potatoes from the bowls and flip the parcel over onto a serving plate. Serve hot.

Serves 4–6   Preparation time: 55 mins   Cooking time: 25 mins

Bean Sprouts with Salted Fish

100 g (3¹/₂ oz) dried salted fish,
  soaked, rinsed, patted dry and thinly
  sliced
3 tablespoons oil
5 cloves garlic, sliced
¹/₄ large onion, thinly sliced
1–2 red finger-length chillies, deseeded
  and thinly sliced
3 dried black Chinese mushrooms,
  soaked to soften and sliced (optional)
3 tablespoons oyster sauce
¹/₂ teaspoon sesame oil
1 tablespoon rice wine
300 g (10 oz) bean sprouts
2 spring onions, cut into short lengths
4 stalks garlic chives (koo chye), cut
  into lengths
¹/₄ teaspoon white pepper

1 Heat the oil in a wok over medium heat and stir-fry the salted fish until golden brown and crispy, about 2 minutes. Remove from the oil and set aside to drain.
2 Add the garlic, onion, chillies and mushrooms to the wok and stir-fry over medium heat for 2 minutes. Add the oyster sauce, sesame oil and rice wine, and mix for about 1 minute. Add the bean sprouts, spring onions and chives, increase the heat to high and stir-fry briskly for 2 to 3 minutes. Transfer the vegetables to a serving platter.
3 Season with the pepper and toss well. Then sprinkle the fried salted fish and serve immediately.

Note: Soak the salted fish in water for 10 minutes before frying if the fish is heavily salted.

Serves 4   Preparation time: 20 mins   Cooking time: 10 mins

Kangkung Belachan   Water Spinach Stir-fried with Spicy Prawn Paste

A popular method of cooking this excellent leafy green vegetable using both Malay and Chinese seasonings.

750 g (1¹/₂ lbs) kangkung (water
  spinach), washed and cleaned,
  tough bottom ends of stems and
  wilted leaves discarded
2–3 tablespoons oil
3 tablespoons dried prawns, soaked
  in water to soften, then coarsely
  ground in a mortar or blender
2–4 teaspoons sugar
1 teaspoon sesame oil
1 tablespoon soy sauce
1 red finger-length chilli, thinly sliced
¹/₂ teaspoon salt
¹/₂ teaspoon pepper

Spice Paste
2¹/₂ cm (1 in) fresh ginger, peeled
  and sliced
5–8 red finger-length chillies, deseeded
  and sliced
6 shallots, peeled
6 cloves garlic, peeled
2 teaspoons belachan (dried prawn
  paste)

1 Use only the tender tips and leaves of the kangkung, and discard the tough stems. Wash the leaves and stems thoroughly in several changes of water to remove any grit.
2 To prepare the Spice Paste, grind the ingredients in a mortar or blender, adding a little oil if necessary to keep the blades turning.
3 Heat the oil in a wok and stir-fry the ground dried prawns and the Spice Paste over medium heat for 5 to 7 minutes until fragrant. Add the sugar, sesame oil, soy sauce and sliced chilli, and stir to mix well. Increase the heat to high, add the kangkung and stir-fry briskly until the vegetable is slightly wilted, about 3 minutes. Season with the salt and pepper. Best served hot.

Serves 6   Preparation time: 20 mins   Cooking time: 10 mins

Mild Potato Curry with Yogurt

5 cloves garlic
3 cm (1$^1/_4$ in) fresh ginger, peeled
  and sliced
3 tablespoons oil
1 large onion, sliced
2 tablespoons ground coriander
1 tablespoon chilli powder
1 teaspoon ground turmeric
1 teaspoon ground cumin
2 cloves
1 cinnamon stick
1 sprig curry leaves
750 g (1$^1/_2$ lbs) potatoes, peeled and
  cut into chunks
2 tomatoes, cut into wedges
2 cups (500 ml) water
2 teaspoons freshly squeezed lime
  or lemon juice
6 sprigs coriander leaves (cilantro),
  coarsely chopped
1$^1/_2$ teaspoons salt
$^1/_4$ teaspoon pepper
1$^1/_2$ teaspoons sugar
1 cup (250 ml) plain yogurt

1 Grind the garlic and ginger to a paste in a mortar.
2 Heat the oil in a wok over medium heat and stir-fry the onion until golden, about 5 minutes. Add the garlic-ginger paste, all the spices and the curry leaves, and continue to stir-fry gently for 4 to 5 minutes.
3 Add the potatoes and stir-fry until they are well-coated with the spices, about 1 minute. Then add the tomatoes and water, and simmer, covered, stirring occasionally until the potatoes are cooked, about 15 to 20 minutes minutes.
4 Add the lime juice and coriander leaves, and mix well. Season with the salt, pepper and sugar. Swirl in the yogurt and remove from the heat. Serve immediately with rice or bread.

Serves 4–6   Preparation time: 25 mins   Cooking time: 35 mins

Eggplant Masala

3 tablespoons oil
1 teaspoon mustard seeds
$^1/_2$ teaspoon cumin seeds
1 onion, sliced
4 cloves garlic, sliced
2 slender Asian eggplants (500 g/1 lb
  total), halved and cut into lengths
1 teaspoon chilli powder
1 teaspoon ground coriander
$^1/_2$ teaspoon ground turmeric
$^1/_2$ teaspoon salt
2 teaspoons tamarind pulp mashed
  in 4 tablespoons water, squeezed
  and strained to obtain juice

1 Heat the oil in a wok over medium heat and cook the mustard seeds until they pop, about 1 minute. Add the cumin seeds and gently stir-fry for 1 minute. Add the onion and garlic, and stir-fry until light golden brown, about 5 minutes.
2 Add the eggplants, chilli powder, coriander, turmeric and salt, and stir-fry for 1 minute. Then add the tamarind juice, reduce the heat and simmer until the eggplants are tender, about 7 minutes. Serve immediately with freshly cooked rice.

Serves 4–6   Preparation time: 25 mins   Cooking time: 20 mins

Tropical Fruits in Steamed Coconut Custard

These steamed cakes made with jackfruit (or other tropical fruits) make a delicious snack or dessert.

1 cup (150 g) rice flour
$^1/_2$ cup (60 g) tapioca starch
3 cups (750 ml) thin coconut milk or
  1 cup (250 ml) coconut cream
  mixed with 2 cups (500 ml) water
$^1/_2$ teaspoon salt
3 pandanus leaves, tied in a knot,
  or $^1/_4$ teaspoon pandanus essence
1$^1/_2$ cups (200 g) diced jackfruit or
  mango or sliced banana
16 pieces banana leaf, each about
  20-cm (8-in) square
$^1/_2$ cup (125 ml) coconut cream
$^1/_2$ cup (125 ml) Palm Sugar Syrup
  (page 73)

1 Prepare the Palm Sugar Syrup by following the instructions on page 73.
2 Combine the rice flour, tapioca starch, coconut milk, salt and pandanus leaves or essence in a saucepan, and cook over very low heat, stirring constantly, until the creamy mixture becomes very thick, about 10 minutes. Remove from the heat and discard the pandanus leaves (if using). Allow the mixture to cool, then add the fruit and mix well.
3 Place one piece of banana leaf on top of another and spoon 2 tablespoons of the cooked mixture onto the centre, then spoon $^1/_2$ tablespoon each of the coconut cream and Palm Sugar Syrup over the mixture. Fold two opposite sides of the banana leaves over the filling so they overlap each other, then seal the two ends with toothpicks.
4 Alternatively, roll the banana leaf into a cone and spoon 2 tablespoons of the cooked mixture into it (see photo). Serve the coconut cream and Palm Sugar Syrup in small bowls on the side.
5 Steam the bundles for 25 minutes in a bamboo steamer or on a steaming tray inside a covered wok. Remove from the steamer and allow to cool to room temperature or chill before serving.

Serves 4–6   Preparation time: 15 mins   Cooking time: 35 mins

Coconut Mango Pudding

Delicate and light, garnish these simple puddings with fresh mango and other fruits to create an elegant dessert.

4 cups (1 litre) water
$^1/_2$ cup (125 g) sugar
2 tablespoons gelatine powder
1 cup (250 ml) thick coconut milk or
  $^1/_2$ cup (125 ml) coconut cream
  mixed with $^1/_2$ cup (125 ml) water
$^1/_2$ cup (125 ml) fresh milk
2 eggs, beaten
1 large mango (about 450 g), peeled,
  pitted and puréed
1 large mango (about 450 g), peeled,
  pitted and diced
1 large mango (about 450 g), peeled,
  pitted and sliced to garnish
Strawberries, kiwi or other fruits, to
  garnish (optional)

1 Combine the water, sugar and gelatine powder in a saucepan and stir constantly over low heat until the sugar and gelatine is completely dissolved, about 7 to 10 minutes.
2 Remove from the heat, add the coconut milk or cream, fresh milk, eggs and mango purée, and mix well. Then add the diced mango and mix again.
3 Pour the mixture into small moulds and refrigerate until set. Garnish with the sliced mango, strawberries and kiwis or other fruits (if using) and serve.

Serves 4–6   Preparation time: 25 mins   Cooking time: 10 mins

Chilled Almond Jelly with Lychees or Longans

A classic Chinese restaurant dish that is very easy to make and can be prepared well in advance. What a great way to end a Chinese dinner!

3 cups (750 ml) water
2 tablespoons agar-agar powder
1 cup (250 ml) fresh milk
1/2 cup (125 g) sugar
2 teaspoons almond essence
One (600-g/20-oz) can lychees
  or longans, with canning syrup,
  chilled
Ice cubes (optional)

1 Pour the water into a deep saucepan and sprinkle the agar-agar powder over it. Stir gently and slowly bring to a boil over medium heat. Then reduce the heat and simmer gently over low heat for 5 minutes. Add the milk and sugar, and continue to stir until the sugar is completely dissolved. Then add the almond essence and gently simmer for another minute. Pour the mixture into a square or rectangular dish and leave to set, then refrigerate until required.
2 Just before serving, pour the chilled lychees or longans and their canning syrup into a large bowl. Cut the almond jelly into squares and add to the bowl. Add a few ice cubes, if desired, and serve immediately.

Serves 4–6   Preparation time: 5 mins   Cooking time: 15 mins

Sweet Red Beans with Coconut Cream

This favourite Chinese dessert is believed to be very nutritious. As it is quite filling, it is sometimes served as a snack between meals or with afternoon tea.

1 cup (200 g) dried red adzuki beans
  (see note), soaked in water for 1–2
  hours, then drained
4 cups (1 litre) water
3/4 cup (150 g) sugar
5 pandanus leaves, tied in a knot
  or 1/2 teaspoon pandanus essence
1/2 cup (125 ml) coconut cream

1 Cover the drained adzuki beans with the water in a pot and bring to a boil. Reduce the heat and simmer over low heat, uncovered, for 40 minutes until the beans are very soft.
2 Add the sugar and pandanus leaves or essence, stir gently and cook for another 10 minutes. Remove from the heat and discard the pandanus leaves, if using. Ladle the sweetened beans into individual bowls and serve warm, topped with a swirl of fresh coconut cream.

Note: Do not confuse small red adzuki beans with the much larger red kidney beans which do not work as well for this recipe. Adzuki beans are sold dried and need to be soaked before using. Cooked, sweetened adzuki beans are available canned in supermarkets.

Serves 4–6   Preparation time: 15 mins   Cooking time: 50 mins

Gula Melaka   Sago Pearls with Coconut Milk and Palm Sugar

Smooth sago pearls bathed in creamy coconut cream and golden brown Palm Sugar Syrup make this one of Singapore's best-loved desserts. The name literally means "Malacca Sugar", although any type of palm sugar (also known as *gula merah* or "red sugar") or maple syrup may be used.

$1^1/_2$ cups (150 g) dried sago pearls
  (see note)
$^1/_4$ teaspoon pandanus essence or
  3 pandanus leaves, tied in a knot
12 cups (3 litres) water
1 cup (250 ml) Palm Sugar Syrup
  (see note on page 73)
$1^1/_2$ cups (375 ml) coconut cream
Crushed ice, to serve (optional)

1 Rinse the sago pearls and place in a pot with the pandanus essence or pandanus leaves. Add the water and bring to a boil, stirring constantly for 15 minutes. If using pandanus leaves, remove and discard them. Remove the pot from the heat, cover and set aside for 5 minutes.

2 Drain the sago pearls, discarding the water. Rinse the sago under cold running water and drain again. Spoon the sago pearls into individual serving bowls and refrigerate until set.

3 To serve, drizzle Palm Sugar Syrup and coconut cream over the sago and top with crushed ice, if desired.

Note: Dried sago pearls are white pearls of sago starch. They must be rinsed in water and drained to remove excess starch before use. When cooked, they are transparent and have little taste. Sold in the dried form in grocery stores.

Serves 6–8   Preparation time: 5 mins   Cooking time: 20 mins

Sago with Honeydew and Coconut Milk

7 tablespoons dried sago pearls (see
  note above)
9 cups ($2^1/_2$ litres) water
$^1/_2$ cup (100 g) sugar
1 ripe honeydew melon, or cantaloupe
$1^1/_2$ cups (375 ml) coconut cream
Crushed ice, to serve (optional)

1 Rinse the sago pearls, place in a pot with 8 cups (2 litres) water and bring to a boil, stirring constantly for 15 minutes. Remove the pot from the heat, cover and set aside for 5 minutes. Drain the sago pearls, discarding the water. Rinse the sago under cold running water, drain again and set aside.

2 Boil the sugar and $^1/_2$ cup (125 ml) water to make a sugar syrup. Remove from the heat and set aside to cool.

3 Halve the honeydew or cantaloupe, then peel and deseed. Blend half the melon flesh in a juicer or process in a blender with $^1/_2$ cup (125 ml) water. Cube the other half of the melon flesh or shape into balls with a small melon baller. Mix the cooked sago pearls, coconut cream, honeydew juice and cubes, and drizzle a little sugar syrup over to taste. Serve well chilled with crushed ice, if desired.

Serves 6–8   Preparation time: 25 mins   Cooking time: 15 mins

Measurements and conversions

Measurements in this book are given in volume as far as possible. Teaspoon, tablespoon and cup measurements should be level, not heaped, unless otherwise indicated. Australian readers please note that the standard Australian measuring spoon is larger than the UK or American spoon by 5 ml, so use $^3/_4$ tablespoon instead of a full tablespoon when following the recipes.

Liquid Conversions

Imperial	Metric	US cups
$^1/_2$ fl oz	15 ml	1 tablespoon
1 fl oz	30 ml	$^1/_8$ cup
2 fl oz	60 ml	$^1/_4$ cup
3 fl oz	85 ml	$^1/_3$ cup
4 fl oz	125 ml	$^1/_2$ cup
5 fl oz	150 ml	$^2/_3$ cup
6 fl oz	175 ml	$^3/_4$ cup
8 fl oz	250 ml	1 cup
12 fl oz	375 ml	$1^1/_2$ cups
16 fl oz	500 ml	2 cups
1 quart	1 litre	4 cups

Note:
1 UK pint = 20 fl oz
1 US pint = 16 fl oz

Solid Weight Conversions

Imperial	Metric
$^1/_2$ oz	15 g
1 oz	28 g
$1^1/_2$ oz	45 g
2 oz	60 g
3 oz	85 g
$3^1/_2$ oz	100 g
4 oz ($^1/_4$ lb)	125 g
5 oz	150 g
6 oz	175 g
7 oz	200 g
8 oz ($^1/_2$ lb)	225 g
9 oz	260 g
10 oz	300 g
16 oz (1 lb)	450 g
32 oz (2 lbs)	900 g
$2^1/_4$ lbs	1 kg

Oven Temperatures

Heat	Fahrenheit	Centigrade/Celsius	British Gas Mark
Very cool	230	110	$^1/_4$
Cool or slow	275–300	135–150	1–2
Moderate	350	180	4
Hot	425	220	7
Very hot	450	230	8

Index of recipes

The Tuttle Story

Many people are surprised to learn that the world's largest publisher of books on Asia had its humble beginnings in the tiny American state of Vermont. The company's founder, Charles E. Tuttle, belonged to a New England family steeped in publishing.

Immediately after WW II, Tuttle served in Tokyo under General Douglas MacArthur and was tasked with reviving the Japanese publishing industry. He later founded the Charles E. Tuttle Publishing Company, which thrives today as one of the world's leading independent publishers.

Though a westerner, Tuttle was hugely instrumental in bringing a knowledge of Japan and Asia to a world hungry for information about the East. By the time of his death in 1993, Tuttle had published over 6,000 books on Asian culture, history and art—a legacy honored by the Japanese emperor with the "Order of the Sacred Treasure," the highest tribute Japan can bestow upon a non-Japanese.

With a backlist of 1,500 titles, Tuttle Publishing is more active today than at any time in its past—inspired by Charles Tuttle's core mission to publish fine books to span the East and West and provide a greater understanding of each.